ALSO BY JAMES C. HUMES

Sweet Dream: Tales of a River City

Podium Humor

Roles Speakers Play

How to Get Invited to the White House

Talk Your Way to the Top

Speaker's Treasury of Anecdotes About the Famous

Primary (with John LeBoutillier)

Churchill: Speaker of the Century

Standing Ovation

Instant Eloquence

The Sir Winston Method

The Ben Franklin Factor

Citizen Shakespeare

More Podium Humor

The Wit & Wisdom of Winston Churchill

My Fellow Americans

The Wit & Wisdom of Benjamin Franklin

The Wit & Wisdom of Abraham Lincoln

Confessions of a White House Ghostwriter

Nixon's Ten Commandments of Statecraft

JAMES C. HUMES

SCRIBNER

SCRIBNER

1230 Avenue of the Americas
New York, NY 10020

Copyright © 1997 by James Humes
All rights reserved, including the right of reproduction
in whole or in part in any form.

SCRIBNER and design are trademarks
of Simon & Schuster Inc.

Designed by Brooke Zimmer
Set in Baskerville
Manufactured in the United States of America

1 3 5 7 9 10 8 6 4 2

Library of Congress Cataloging-in-Publication Data
Humes, James C.
Nixon's ten commandments of statecraft : his guiding
principles of leadership and negotiation with commentary
and lessons from history / James Humes.
p.   cm.
Includes index.
1. Nixon, Richard M. (Richard Milhous), 1913–1994—
Views on negotiation. 2. Nixon, Richard M. (Richard
Milhous), 1913–1994 —Views on political leadership.
3. Negotiation—Quotations, maxims, etc. 4. Political
leadership—Quotations, maxims, etc. 5. Diplomacy—
Quotations, maxims, etc. I. Title.
E856.H86   1997
973.924´092—dc21   97-17420
CIP
ISBN 0-684-83795-1

To Ray Price,
R. N.'s intellectual alter ego

ACKNOWLEDGMENTS

I am indebted to many:

To my son-in-law, Cecil Quillen, who has read literally hundreds of historical biographies and who helped me come up with the idea of this book during a lunch on Boxing Day.

To Charles Scribner, like his father, one of the great gentlemen of the publishing world—who made the idea of this book a reality.

To Gillian Blake, my editor, whose pointed questions and helpful suggestions refined and polished my manuscript into a book to be proud of.

To Nancy Kowalchik, for deciphering and typing my writing hieroglyphic into the manuscript.

To Dr. Harvey Sicherman, the head of the Foreign Policy Institute in Philadelphia, a gentleman and scholar who suggested many of the historical parallels during our cigar-puffing discussions at the Union League in Philadelphia.

To Peter Rodman of the Nixon Center for Peace and Freedom in Washington for his assistance.

To Dr. John Lukacs, a distinguished historian who suggested the chapter on General Santa Anna as an example of self-destructive bellicosity (or belligerence—whichever you choose).

To John Taylor, the dynamic leader of the Nixon Library and Museum in Yorba Linda, California, for his encouragement and support.

To my friend, former British Cabinet member Jonathan Aitken, whose biography of President Nixon presents the most accurate portrayal.

And to my many friends—too numerous to mention in full—who remained staunch loyalists of R. N. throughout his life.

And to Julia Rota, who delved into dusty tomes to come up with historical parallels.

To Congressman John LeBoutillier, Donald Baldwin, Elliott Curson, Don Whitehead, to Judge William Vogel and his wife Sara, Susy Brandt, John Price, Tom Evans, James Ring, General Charles West, to Dr. Stuart and Dr. Claire Fox, Ambassador Faith Whittlesey, Ambassador Richard McCormack, Eliska Hasek Coolidge, John McClaughry, Dr. Dick Eisenbeis, Jane Krumrine, Ralph Hooper, Richard Henderson, Sally Cooke, Lee Lansberry, Allen Simpson, Peggy Lindemuth, Diana Atwood Reilly, Perrin Hamilton, Howard Butcher, Nancy Longstreth, John Bennison, Annie Voelker Gladys, Long Frazier, Permar Richards, Jean Tomlinson, Jean Humes, Bob and Barbara Barrows, and my brother Graham.

CONTENTS

Nixon's Ten Commandments of Statecraft

INTRODUCTION

On October 31, 1994, my daughter Mary gave me a dinner party at the Colony Club in New York to celebrate my sixtieth birthday. That night I received from Ed and Tricia Nixon Cox a note card found in President Nixon's shallow desk drawer at his home in Saddle River after his death. The laminated piece, printed on both sides—not too much larger than a calling card—was, upon opening the drawer, immediately visible. It read:

> A President needs a global view, a sense of proportion and a keen sense of the possible. He needs to know how power operates and he must have the will to use it.
> If I could carve ten rules into the walls of the Oval Office for my successors in the dangerous years just ahead, they would be these. . . .

Nixon then listed the rules that I have called the Ten Commandments of Statecraft.

My family's connection with the Nixons began in 1952 when my mother wired a telegram and money order to the

Republican National Committee after she heard Senator Nixon's defense to charges of maintaining a secret fund.

Nixon sent a note back to my mother, which I found when my mother died in 1955. A month later, when I was visiting friends in the Spring Valley section of Washington, I took the note—and a steak bone for Checkers, the beloved cocker spaniel—to the Nixon home across the street. That was the first time that I ever met Richard Nixon. He thanked me and then asked if I, too, was a Republican.

In early 1958, my wife, Dianne, was working at the White House in the Appointments Office. She had been recruited from the Foreign Service, which she had entered a year after she graduated from Wellesley. Her boss, Bob Gray, asked her to locate a "message writer" for Vice President Nixon. Such a writer drafts telegrams to be read to conventions, notes of commendations to be sent to heroes, and condolence letters to be forwarded to widows of the eminent. Dianne "appointed" herself.

At this time, while Vice President Nixon was gearing up for his 1960 campaign, I was attending George Washington University Law School. I met and talked to Mr. Nixon at the various receptions he gave for his vice presidential staff at his Tudor-style house on Forest Lane.

Most politicians are masters at "schmoozing," but grow guarded when the topic turns from the superficial to the substantial. Nixon was the opposite. One time I asked him what he thought of Franklin Roosevelt. His reply was "Great president, not so much for his principles as his presence," and he continued to discuss the positive attributes and flaws of FDR. Casual chitchat bored Nixon. His real enjoyment came when such occasions became catalysts for new insights or ideas. I remember one time at a New Year's Day reception when he grilled me on how Churchill drafted speeches. (I told Nixon that he dictated them and had them typed in phrases of rough verse form instead of article style.)

In 1958, I started off a conversation with Nixon by saying, "The root of your problems with the eastern establishment was that you were right about Alger Hiss." Nixon nodded his agreement and asked if I would submit a paper to him on the subject, and I did. Thereafter, while my wife worked full-time, I handled various assignments on a part-time basis and attended law school. My chief contribution was compiling a storehouse of quotations and historical anecdotes for use in speeches. Nixon particularly enjoyed my file of "cross-quotes," in which liberals or Democrats criticized John Kennedy or advocated conservative positions (e.g., Eleanor Roosevelt: "I wish Senator Kennedy would show less profile and more courage"; Harry Truman: "Jack Kennedy doesn't know a damn thing about foreign policy").

At Nixon's funeral, Winton "Red" Blount, who served in the Nixon cabinet, sat behind Dianne and me. He tapped me on the shoulder and introduced himself saying, "I don't know your name but I remember the President saying, 'Mr. Postmaster General, this is my Quotes-Master General.' "

I first began assembling my notebooks of quotations for my use as a future politician. (I would serve in the Pennsylvania State General Assembly in the early 1960s.) During the Nixon administration, I was a White House speechwriter and then director of Policy and Plans in Public Affairs at the State Department. My role was to articulate and sell the Nixon Doctrine by both drafting and delivering speeches on his policy for gradual withdrawal of U.S. troops in Asia.

In the years following his resignation, I visited with him many times, once in San Clemente in 1978, when I urged him to make his return to the public arena in Europe, especially England, where his prestige as a statesman was still high. My argument to him was that those abroad view a president through a foreign policy prism and that former prime ministers I had talked to, such as Anthony Eden and Alec Douglas-Home, communicated the regard in which he was held for his wisdom and experience in international affairs. But mostly our relationship was maintained by letter or fax.

The older Nixon grew, the more he hoarded his private time. Yet that in no way diminished the volume of letters and notes he would write to friends. He would, for example, send gifts to my daughters on their college graduations. Nixon disdained the meaningless receptions and social calls that robbed him of the time he could spend on writing books, drafting memoranda to people in government, and counseling visiting foreign leaders, but he would make time for the bright and studious, such as young journalists or students of government. I remember one young Williams graduate who told me after a visit, "What a warm, kind man Mr. Nixon was. I learned more from him than in my years of political science at Williams." Nixon enjoyed exchanges with curious minds who were young enough not to be biased by events of the past and who might shape policy in the future.

He also relished intellectual challenge. He would respond to any policy idea or critique of a government action with prompt observations and detailed evaluations of the points. When I sent him my Churchill biography in 1980, he sent back his comments and then recommended that I write another biography on Bourke Cockran, the Irish-American politician who, according to a conversation Nixon once had with Churchill, molded Churchill's style of speaking. He even wrote the foreword for the book that I am now finishing with the tentative title *Bourke Cockran: The Orator Who Inspired Churchill*.

If someone asked me to help him arrange a meeting with the former president, I would suggest that he write up an outline on what issue he or she wished to discuss (e.g., the Catholic Church and Lech Walesa or investment opportunities in the People's Republic of China). Then I would ask some friend of mine who had particular knowledge of that subject to assist me in writing the letter to Nixon. The letter would discuss the subject matter the prospective caller wanted to cover, as well as possible questions Mr. Nixon might want to ask him. He would screen meetings with strangers, not because he begrudged such visits, but because he wanted to extract the most from the sessions. Meeting a new person was like opening a new book he had ordered, and his intellectual curiosity radiated a warmth.

In 1977, after he had finished his memoirs, Nixon moved to New York City from his exile in San Clemente. The city, he once told me, was "where the action was." There he could meet for quiet discussions with visiting statesmen, aspiring presidential candidates, and foreign policy academics. These meetings took place in his New York apartment until 1982, when he and Mrs. Nixon moved to Saddle River, New Jersey.

During those years, Nixon wrote a series of short books on foreign policy and world affairs in which he was assisted by Ray Price, a former White House speechwriter who was Nixon's intellectual alter ego.

The Ten Commandments of Statecraft were first written in *The Real War.* They were the distillation of his foreign policy experience in the Oval Office. The Ten Commandments are the conclusions of a man whose span of influence in the world's affairs exceeds anyone else's in American history; from the time in 1947 when he served as congressman on the Herter Committee to study the need for foreign aid to Europe, to 1994 when he met with Soviet chairman Boris Yeltsin a few weeks before his death. No one else had ever traveled to as many nations in official capacity—both as vice president and as president—or met more world leaders.

In the Richard Nixon Museum and Library at Yorba Linda, two displays underscore the breadth of his experience. The first is of five statues—Winston Churchill, Charles de Gaulle, Konrad Adenauer, Golda Meir, and Chou En-lai—five giants whom Nixon had known and worked with firsthand. The second is the wall mounting of sixty-nine *Time* magazine covers on which he was featured in a period of almost five decades.

Nixon was aware that the greatest political leaders of this century, such as Churchill and de Gaulle, did their own writing. Nixon did call on speechwriters, but the final product was his own. I recall one speech to the Air Force Academy that went through seven drafts. The final wording was about 80 percent Nixon.

White House speechwriters, in comparing Nixon, Ford, and Reagan, used to say: "Nixon edited substance, Reagan style, and Ford took it as you wrote it." For a major address, Nixon would either write out the rough draft in longhand on his yellow legal pad or enumerate in extensive notes to the speechwriter the points he wanted to cover. He had contempt for those politicians who would read the speeches prepared for them for the first time in their hotel room before they descended to make their talk in the ballroom. "Principles," he once told me, "are not picked out like Calvin Klein ties that can be discarded when they are out of fashion. They are tools of policy that can only be hammered out on the anvil of hard deliberation." Nixon's rules of statecraft gleam like gems in their simple balance of phrasing. The aphorisms are the results of hours spent in reading, reflection, and rewriting.

No other statesman has left a legacy of laws for the conduct of foreign policy. Machiavelli, the author of *The Prince*, that Renaissance dispenser of wisdom on leadership, was not a prince, but an observer of Cesare Borgia. The one exception might be Mao. Yet Mao dismissed *The Little Red Book* as super-ficial when Nixon complimented him on it in Beijing in 1972. Nixon, however, had been impressed by its pungency, if not its philosophy. *The Little Red Book* was not so much a code book for leaders, but a catechism for the masses—and it was written mostly before he assumed full power, not afterward. Churchill and de Gaulle did not write manuals for leadership, but insights can be gleaned from their writings, which Nixon stud-ied. For Nixon, most novels were a waste of time. (He did, however, read Dostoevsky's *The Idiot* before going to Moscow in 1972.) He preferred biographies like Carl Sandburg's *Abra-ham Lincoln,* or histories, such as Churchill's massive accounts of the First and Second World Wars, and Will Durant's series of books on ancient civilizations. One contemporary historian that Nixon recommended I read was the former British Marx-ist Paul Johnson, who wrote *Modern Times.* When Nixon sought escape, he turned not to books but to baseball.

Leaders who shaped history fascinated Nixon. In fact, he wrote a book about those he knew personally entitled *Leaders.* He recognized that he too would have a place in history, and in his postpresidential years, he was determined that his achievements would not go unspotlighted. In 1975, when I vis-ited him in San Clemente, he asked me, "How do you think I shall be regarded in history?" I answered, "Foreign policy achievements are writ large on the pages of history—look at Truman—his domestic scandals diminished with time." "Per-haps," he said, "but it depends on who's writing the history." I later sent him a note saying that a bill of impeachment of President Truman had been introduced in the House. His attorney general, Howard McGrath, had been indicted; mem-bers of the White House staff, as well as the head of the IRS, went to jail; and he left the White House in 1953 with lower approval ratings than Nixon had when he resigned in 1974.

Years earlier, in 1968, after his victory but before his inauguration, his interest in molding history's account of his future administration was indicated when he asked me to read other presidents' memoirs. I told him that Grant's was the best, because his account, written in simple, soldierlike prose, was more than a chronicle. It offered implicitly some critical analyses of leadership. Although Nixon had read the memoirs of recent presidents such as Wilson, Hoover, and Eisenhower, he sought the advice and comments of earlier presidents' books.

In 1991, I sent him a copy of my book *"My Fellow Americans": Presidential Addresses That Shaped History.* The speech that fascinated him the most was George Washington's farewell address, because it was, in a sense, an attempt to shape future American diplomacy. Alexander Hamilton, who admired Frederick the Great, had modeled the draft he wrote for Washington's last presidential address after Frederick's writings, in which he sought to guide Prussian foreign policy from his grave. Hamilton even had a bust of Frederick the Great in his New York City home beside his desk.

Mr. Nixon would write the foreword for my book *The Wit and Wisdom of Winston Churchill,* published in 1994 just before his death. Nixon wrote, "Churchill was the largest human being of all time." But in my talks with him, what drew Nixon to Churchill was the historian as politician. To quote Nixon's foreword, "Churchill is one of the few statesmen who occupied both the world of thought and the world of action." Nixon was skeptical of the conclusions by academics who had no practical experience, just as he was of politicians who had no knowledge of history.

The greatest American maxim writer in history was Benjamin Franklin, and Nixon would have approved of this Franklin nugget: "Diplomacy depends more on what we do than what we say." Actually, Franklin's homely wisdom was written before he entered public affairs, under the pseudonym of Richard Saunders (Poor Richard), and it was intended to liven up the copy of an almanac for farmers on weather and crops.

The American statesmen, however, who most fascinated Nixon were Woodrow Wilson and Theodore Roosevelt, probably for the role they played in world affairs. Wilson was his first political hero. During his formative years, Nixon, raised in a Quaker family, was inspired by Wilson's vision of a world peace that would be guaranteed by a League of Nations based on self-determination. In his Executive Office building hideaway, Nixon would proudly point out that his desk was Wilson's desk. (When aides later found out that it belonged to Henry Wilson, Wilson's secretary of labor, they were afraid to tell Nixon the truth.)

Later, Vice President Nixon, at the urging of his friend Alice Roosevelt Longworth, the former president's daughter, became the head of the Theodore Roosevelt Centennial Commission. At that time, Nixon read the Hermann Hagedorn biography of the Republican Roosevelt, as well as a collection of TR's quotations, which the Centennial Commission published. Theodore Roosevelt's blunt exercise of Realpolitik might seem more suited to Nixon than the moralistic idealism of Wilson, but in personal terms, Nixon identified far more with the academic and introverted Wilson than with the boisterous and theatrical TR. On the political front, both presidents won Nobel Peace Prizes, but Nixon would point out that the hardheaded Roosevelt had more success in ending the Russo-Japanese War in the 1905 Portsmouth (New Hampshire) Conference than the visionary Wilson in the Versailles Treaty in 1919.

Pop psychologists—whom Nixon abhorred—might try to compare the personalities of Wilson to that of his mother, Hannah, the Sunday school–teaching Quaker, and Theodore Roosevelt to his father, Frank, the argumentative extrovert who never held back his opinions, even to paying customers in his store. In fact, Nixon's brother Edward once said to me, "Dick had a lot of his mother's ideals, but his love of debate he might have gotten from our father."

Edward Nixon also told me that Nixon's thirst to see the world began when he was a child. The train whistle that Nixon talked about in his 1968 convention acceptance speech was a siren inviting dreams to visit faraway places. The Pacific Ocean that lapped its waves near his Yorba Linda home sparked an early interest in the nation that lay on the other side. Later, his naval duty in the South Pacific in World War II most certainly heightened his interest in Asia.

Yet it was the world on this side of the Atlantic that would be the prime interest of Congressman Nixon in 1947 right after the war. Congressman Christian Herter (who would later succeed John Foster Dulles as secretary of state in 1959) tapped Nixon to serve on a select committee studying war-ravaged Europe to see if the massive foreign aid plans proposed by Secretary of State George Marshall were justified. Herter told me in 1960 that he chose the freshman Nixon because he was an internationalist Republican from the West rather than the East Coast. Nixon, he said, had turned out to be "the workhorse on the committee." Unlike others, Herter explained, Nixon did not seek the nightlife of Paris. He stayed in his hotel room every night poring over reports assessing the devastating economic effects of the war. In the language of the nineties, he was a "policy wonk."

The two looming giants in Europe in those early postwar years were Churchill and de Gaulle; even though their careers had been temporarily sidetracked—Churchill lost the prime ministership in 1945, and de Gaulle resigned as provisional head of government when the French politicians failed to restructure its weak parliamentary government.

Nixon first met Churchill in June 1954, when he greeted the Prime Minister upon his arrival in Washington. He was "amazed that the seventy-nine-year-old man who had recently suffered a stroke, who had just crossed the Atlantic on an overnight prop plane ride, could have covered so many subjects so well in the thirty minutes it took us to reach the White House. And all the time he talked, he continually waved to the crowds that lined the route."

In 1957, Churchill was the speaker at the American Bar Association meeting in London. He told Charles Rhyne—a Duke law school classmate of Nixon and then leader of the ABA—that Nixon, in his meetings with him as vice president, was the best-briefed and best-prepared spokesman for the American government he had ever encountered. Churchill also lauded Nixon for his answers in a press conference on foreign policy following a memorial service he attended at St. Paul's Cathedral in 1957. "The proof of his success," said Churchill, "was the standing ovation by reporters at the conclusion of the questioning."

De Gaulle, however, occupied a special niche in the ranks of Nixon heroes. In 1963, when the out-of-office Nixon traveled on business to France, the U.S. Embassy in Paris refused to offer their customary good offices to a former vice president. Despite the embassy's deliberate snub, President de Gaulle hosted a dinner for Nixon, in which he toasted Nixon's eventual return to national leadership.

Nixon studied the lives of both Churchill and de Gaulle carefully. In Nixon's last public address, he would quote them both: "We all remember what Churchill said about democracy, that it 'is the worst form of government except for all those other forms that have been tried from time to time.' Well, perhaps capitalism is the worst economic system except for every other form that's been tried from time to time." Later in that final talk, he cited his favorite de Gaulle quotation, which originated from Sophocles: "We have to wait until the evening sunset to see how glorious the day has been."

In 1982, when I was a Woodrow Wilson Fellow at the Center for International Scholars at the Smithsonian, I attended a dinner where retired British prime minister Harold Macmillan delivered some short, informal remarks. Afterward, he regaled a few of us with an anecdote about Churchill:

"In early 1942—when, frankly, the Allies were not winning the war—I was resident minister in Algiers. One night in Morocco, I was taken aback by Churchill's question, 'Harold, what do you think of Cromwell?' I ventured the opinion, 'He was a rather aggressive man, wasn't he, Prime Minister?' Looking stern, Churchill answered, 'Harold, Cromwell was obsessed with Spain, but he never saw the danger of France.' "

Macmillan went on to say that Churchill was the only leader in early 1942 who was considering the role the Soviet Union would play in the postwar world. The rest of us, Macmillan explained, were only thinking how we would beat the Nazis, but Churchill, who had already factored in the entry of the United States and the invasion of Russia by Hitler, had deemed the defeat of Germany inevitable and had already turned his thoughts to an imperialist Russia after the war.

In praising Churchill, Macmillan said that the true leader does not just react to prevailing conditions but perceives emerging patterns and how they might shape future political developments and events. He then quoted another Churchill maxim: "Every statesman has to be scientist, historian, and soldier—a scientist to project demographics and statistics into the future, an historian to understand patterns of the past that may soon be replicated, and a soldier who is brave enough to take measures—even if unpopular—to escape looming disaster and enhance the cause of peace."

In the midst of the world war against the Axis, Churchill's remark to Macmillan was a way of saying, in reference to the Soviet Union, "What After the War?" In 1967, Nixon wrote an article for *Foreign Affairs* entitled "What After Viet Nam?" It was written close to two years before he assumed the presidency in 1969, and it gave a hint of his thinking on China. In both cases, Churchill and Nixon were not responding to an immediate crisis. To use a phrase in fashion with business management today, they were not "reactive" but "proactive." In looking back, I recall a conversation with Vice President Nixon that should have given me a clue to his later rapprochement with China. In his home in Forest Lane, I heard him say, "Someday I will visit China."

"You mean Formosa?" I asked.

"No, China," he answered curtly. "Mainland China." At the same time, incidentally, he described Generalissimo Chiang Kai-shek as a man of limited intelligence. "The brains," he said, "are with his wife."

Some decades later, after he delivered one of his *tour d'horizon* talks, using neither lectern nor notes, on world affairs to a private audience at Philadelphia's Union League, he displayed that Churchillian combination of scientist, historian, and soldier. When asked to explain his decision to open relations with China, he explained that statistically, he saw the expanding population explosion of China and what it would mean economically in future markets and trade, and geopolitically, how our access with the People's Republic would strengthen our international leverage. He cited some comments made by historian Paul Johnson describing how Rome had recognized the Celtic tribes of Gaul and Britain and had absorbed them into the Empire but had spurned trading with the Germanic tribes, snubbing them as "barbarians" who did not appreciate the superiority of Roman civilization. But it was the Germans, said Nixon, led by Alaric, who would virtually destroy the Roman Empire and thrust Europe into the Dark Ages.

Nixon added that, for most politicians, "Vision is the answer to yesterday's headlines." In his book *Leaders,* he describes the difference between those who are leaders and those who are mere managers. "Management is prose; leadership is poetry; the manager thinks of today; the leader must think of the day after tomorrow."

Vision, to Nixon, was knowledge of the past directed toward the future. Like too few politicians today, Nixon was a student of history. One example of this was the essay he wrote for the New York Bar Association exam, which he had to pass when he moved to New York in 1963 to practice law. Board members said later it was the best examination paper they had ever read.

On a question asking him to explain the U.S. Constitution, he wrote, the Constitution "is a series of balances—first, between the Federal Government and the States, and then between the Executive, Legislative, and Judicial branches, and finally, between freedom and order."

On the separation of powers, Nixon, in a law examination essay, wrote that governments often collapse when one branch grew too powerful—the executive in czarist Russia, the legislative in the revolving parliamentary governments of postwar France, and the judicial with the all-powerful Sanhedrin Court in ancient Israel. Never had a former vice president and presidential candidate taken a law exam. Few lawyers or politicians, if any, would have written such an answer.

It was this knowledge of history, joined with the experience of a half century's involvement in foreign affairs, that would shape his Ten Commandments of Statecraft.

Nixon once pointed out to me a strange painting outside the Oval Office. Most of it—two thirds—was raw, gray canvas. The title of the portrait was *The Signing of the Declaration of Independence*. It depicted a handful of signers in the foreground and then a few penciled sketches. The portrait—commissioned by Congress—was not completed because the artist died before finishing it.

Nixon said, "I keep it there to show visitors that it is not just the signers or statesmen or politicians who are called on to fulfill this promise of America—but all of us—all of us are in the picture.

"The success of democracy, unlike a dictatorship," continued Nixon, "is not measured by one extraordinary man but by the ordinary men doing their jobs extraordinarily well. All of us are in the picture and are called on to be leaders in business, the community, or church."

Similarly, Nixon, in one sense, wrote his Ten Commandments to be pondered by future presidents and leaders. Yet in a larger sense, Nixon wrote these precepts as a guide applicable to all in the role of leadership or management.

I

ALWAYS BE PREPARED TO NEGOTIATE, BUT NEVER NEGOTIATE WITHOUT BEING PREPARED.

Nixon

"Preparation is everything, Jamie—bust your butt!" That was the advice of Vice President Richard Nixon to me as I entered George Washington University Law School.

The maxim Nixon wrote as the first of his Ten Commandments has a more musical lilt. In a sense it echoes the second-best-known line that Ted Sorensen created for Kennedy's inaugural address in 1961: "Never fear to negotiate, but never negotiate out of fear." Nixon was sitting on the inaugural platform as the outgoing Vice President when that memorable phrase was spoken by the man who had recently defeated him.

Nixon may or may not have been familiar with the Benjamin Franklin adage: "To be forewarned is to be forearmed," but he definitely knew and quoted George Washington's advice to his nation in his farewell address: "The only way to ensure peace is to be prepared for war." Even the magnanimous Lincoln said the best negotiation position "is the biggest purse and the longest cannon."

When Nixon first wrote, he may have been referring to a preparedness more national than personal. Yet in Nixon's public life, the physical readiness of a nation and the mental readiness of its leaders were intertwined.

Nixon, who grew up without the advantages of a moneyed background or the charismatic charm of looks and personality, saw preparation as his equalizer.

George Smathers, who was elected to Congress as a returning war veteran in 1946 like Nixon and Kennedy, was a friend of both men and observed their opposite styles when they served on the House Labor and Education Committee. In 1994, Smathers told me that when the two traveled on the same train and stayed in adjoining rooms at hotels, Dick tried hard to be one of the guys. When Jack would tell a dirty story, Dick would laugh even when he didn't understand it. When Jack would be hitting the nightspots, Dick would be hitting the books, boning up "on all those numbers of jobs and employment rates."

It was Congressman Nixon's capacity for drudge work—poring over hearings, transcripts, checking out inconsistencies and reinterviewing witnesses privately—that led him to believe that Alger Hiss was lying. The Republican foreign policy adviser, John Foster Dulles, told him to drop the investigation, as did his fellow Republican on the committee, Karl Mundt. Nixon, however, doggedly pressed on. As he told me once, "The replies of Hiss seemed too crafted and too cute."

The fame he garnered for his role in Hiss's conviction for perjury led first to his Senate victory in 1950, and then to his selection as Eisenhower's running mate in 1952. The general saw Nixon as an internationalist with the anti-Communist credentials to appeal to the Taft wing of the Republican Party. The allegations that Nixon had a secret slush fund made some question his selection as a running mate soon after the convention. It was "secret" only in the sense that Herbert Hoover

Jr., the organizer, did not want Nixon to know the identity of givers and thus be beholden to them. (Governor Adlai Stevenson had a similar fund. He, however, was aware of his donors.)

Because of his television address explaining the Fund, Nixon turned out to be the most press-covered vice president since Theodore Roosevelt in 1900.

Much has been written about Eisenhower's alleged discomfort with Nixon. It is true that Vice President Nixon never became noticeably close to President Eisenhower. Eisenhower's intimates included few who were not his contemporaries and none who were professional politicians. Eisenhower shared the disdain most career military have for career politicians. Still, Eisenhower had enough respect for Nixon's intelligence and judgment to elevate the office of vice president to an influential role in government. Only two decades had passed since the Vice President was ridiculed as Mr. Throttlebottom in the musical *Of Thee I Sing*. Eisenhower would make his vice president "deputy chief of state" as well as "deputy head of party." In the latter, Nixon was the chief cheerleader for the Republican Party, and as a consequence, collected chits for his presidential run in 1960. By making Nixon his surrogate in foreign visits, Eisenhower gave his vice president foreign policy experience no other vice president ever had.

Nixon relished his role as the President's representative in state visits abroad and as his "ears and eyes" in assessing international conditions. Two vice presidential tours particularly enhanced the American perception of Nixon as a future president. The first was the courage he displayed under fire in the Communist-organized mob violence in Caracas during his South American tour in 1958. The other, and more significant, was his journey to the Soviet Union in 1959.

Officially, the Nixon trip to the Trade Exhibition in Moscow was the reciprocation for Soviet deputy premier Kozlov's visit to Washington the year before. If one definition of statesmanship is the communication and advocacy of policy at the highest diplomatic level, Nixon's meetings with Premier Khrushchev in Moscow qualified as the first serious test of his diplomatic career.

Accordingly, Nixon spent six months preparing himself. Not since his days spent studying for the California Bar exam did Nixon immerse himself with such intensity. He requested and secured classified briefings from the CIA and State Department. With Eisenhower's approval, he called foreign leaders such as Prime Minister Harold Macmillan and Chancellor Konrad Adenauer for their assessments of the Soviet premier. In Washington, he met with Senator Hubert Humphrey, who had once been closeted for two hours with Khrushchev. Nixon also had several discussions with the dying John Foster Dulles at Walter Reed Hospital on his opinions of the Soviet leader. He also invited the dean of American pundits, Walter Lippmann of *The New York Times,* as well as the paper's top foreign news reporter, Turner Catledge, to come to his office, where he probed them to find the real Soviet policy behind the propaganda.

His best source was the Russian-speaking Chip Bohlen, who served as ambassador to Moscow under both Truman and Eisenhower. Bohlen knew the internal politics behind Khrushchev's rise to power in the Kremlin and the cast of rivals that could potentially coalesce against him. Nixon also turned to the Russian specialists in the State Department and to universities such as Georgetown, the University of Pennsylvania's Foreign Policy Institute, and Harvard.

Preemptive nuclear strike and the threat of long-range missiles were just two of the 132 topics that might come up for discussion. Other items included trade, collectivization of the farms, and Soviet weapons systems. Nixon had categorized and amassed a file on each topic in his preparation for the Moscow visit.

Most nights in the spring of 1959, he would lug some of the files to his Forest Lane home in order to commit to memory facts and statistics for any questions the Soviets might pose.

He also asked the Library of Congress to provide him with a reading list that included biographies of Peter the Great, Lenin, Trotsky, Stalin, and the Romanovs, as well as histories of Russia and the Revolution. On these books, he penned notes on his yellow legal pads, which were then typed up.

I can recall Nixon trying out Russian proverbs and amenities on us (*dobri ootrim*—good day) at a reception. One Russian word that triggered a wry comment from Nixon was *mir*, which he noted meant both "world" and "peace." Maybe, he joked, that explains Russia's historic imperialism?

From his readings of Russian history and his talks with those who had taken measure of Soviet leaders at close hand, Nixon realized how important display was to the Russians— whether it was the armed forces the Kremlin assembled on the May Day celebration or the facade that Potemkin once erected to impress Catherine II. When Khrushchev boasted of *Sputnik*, the orbiting rocketry that beat the Americans in the race to space in 1957, or brandished his shoe in a UN tirade in 1959, he revealed the Soviet love of the dramatic gesture. Symbolism was often as powerful as substance to the rulers of the Kremlin.

With this in mind, Nixon had the idea to arrive in a plane that would break the speed record between Washington and Moscow. He asked that the vice presidential party arrive on one of the United States's new 707 superjets.

Yet when he landed, Nixon was greeted with an icy reception by Deputy Premier Kozlov, who was accompanied by only a handful of Soviet officials.

The first meeting between Nixon and Khrushchev was supposed to be simply a protocol formal welcome, but Khrushchev was immediately hostile. Referring to the Captive

Nations resolution that Congress had just passed, Khrushchev, red-faced with rage, bellowed, "It reminds me of a saying among our Russian peasants, that 'people should not go to the toilet where they eat.' This resolution stinks! It stinks like fresh horse shit, and nothing smells worse than that!"

Nixon remembered from his studies that Khrushchev had once worked as a swineherd and hit back, "I am afraid that the Chairman is mistaken. There is something that smells worse than horse shit, and that is pig shit." Khrushchev paused for a moment—taken aback—and then he laughed, dropping the subject of the Captive Nations resolution.

When the two leaders arrived at the American exhibition, Khrushchev played to the television cameras, hectoring Nixon. "You don't know anything about Communism except fear of it." Nixon reacted by gamely adhering to the agreed-upon script that America was a great country because of its free competition and free exchange of ideas.

"Sure, let's compete," replied Khrushchev. "You're the lawyer for capitalism, and I'm the lawyer for Communism."

"The way you dominate the conversation, you would make a good lawyer yourself," retorted Nixon. "If you were in the United States Senate, you would be accused of filibustering. You do all the talking and don't let anyone else talk. To us, democracy is the right to choose, and the fact that we have one thousand builders—building one thousand different houses—that's the most important thing. We don't have one decision made at the top by one government official. That is the difference between the two countries."

By the time the two leaders were coaxed to move to the kitchen by an aggressive public relations agent named Bill Safire, a cool Nixon was more than holding his own against an angry Khrushchev. Harrison Salisbury of *The New York Times* observed, "Nixon couldn't have done it better. He won that debate and shook up the Russians."

In the preliminary negotiating before the trip, the Soviets granted Nixon the opportunity to make one lone television and radio broadcast of a formal speech dedicating the American housing and appliance exhibition, which would then be reprinted in *Pravda*. He began by rebutting the Soviet propaganda line that the model American home was no more typical than the Taj Mahal or Buckingham Palace were typical of average houses in India or Britain. As Jonathan Aitken describes in his biography *Nixon*, he reeled off statistics, without notes, showing that 44 million families owned 56 million cars and 50 million television sets; 31 million owned their own homes, and 25 million of them were larger than the model home in the exhibition. He ended his thirty-minute talk by proclaiming: "We believe that you and all other peoples on this earth should have the right to choose the kind of economic or political system which best fits your particular problems, without any foreign intervention."

Almost thirty years later, according to Aitken, a prominent Soviet engineer, Boris Armanov, recounted his reaction. "We really listened to him, and afterward we argued and argued about why Americans had so much freedom, so much money, and all their truthful newspapers. It was the first time any of our generation considered that the West might have some things in their society which might be good for our country."

In this First Commandment of Statecraft, Nixon may also have been thinking of the national dimensions of preparation; in particular, preparation for a summit meeting.

In a note to me on my Churchill biography, Nixon said the most significant phrase in the Fulton, Missouri, speech was not "an iron curtain has descended across the Continent" but these words: "From what I have seen of our Soviet friends and allies during the war, I am convinced that there is nothing which they admire more than military strength, and nothing for which they have less respect than weakness, particularly military weakness."

Nixon, despite his relish for personal diplomacy, was a skeptic about summitry when he came to the presidency in 1969. True, he had promised in the campaign to meet Chairman Leonid Brezhnev, and he would do so when he deemed the time was right. The Soviets conveyed signals indicating their interest in a summit meeting in his first year, but for Nixon, the idea of a meeting with Brezhnev had to be put on a back burner.

Nixon viewed recent summit meetings, such as that between Kennedy and Khrushchev in Geneva in 1962, and Lyndon Johnson with Brezhnev in Glassboro, New Jersey, in 1967, as disasters. Nixon often related to friends former Secretary Dean Acheson's comment to him that "Khrushchev cleaned Kennedy's clock in Geneva." Acheson had said publicly that Kennedy was "woefully unprepared." In 1966, President Johnson traveled to the little college town of Glassboro, New Jersey, to meet Brezhnev as he came down from New York, where he had just addressed the United Nations. Johnson, in Nixon's opinion, had no clear objective of what the United States should gain from the meeting. The communication was at cross-purposes. Johnson argued for a decrease in offensive missiles and Brezhnev for a limiting of defensive missiles.

Such a summit, replete with photo opportunities of smiles and handshakes, but empty of any substantive agreement, was a diplomatic coup for the Soviets, because the result of these "good feeling" atmospherics was to lull the American people, sapping their resolve and weakening their defense commitment.

Nixon finally came around to the idea of a summit if it impelled serious negotiation in advance of the conference.

But for Nixon, such constructive diplomatic bargaining would occur only if the United States went to the conference table with some heavy cards.

For the summit meeting in the summer of 1972 in Moscow, Nixon had a clear objective: détente (a French word for the easing of tensions between adversaries). The proof that would symbolize this breakthrough in relations with the Soviets would be an arms control agreement—specifically a SALT (Strategic Arms Limitation Talks) agreement with the Soviets. But to Nixon such an accord was not the real purpose of the meeting but a means to an end—détente.

Under Lyndon Johnson and Dean Rusk, Soviet relations had been compartmentalized: their support for North Vietnam, their relationship with Castro, their aggressive moves in the Mideast, and their nuclear armament buildup were seen as separate issues. Nixon demanded "linkage" of these confrontation points. Détente would be judged by the total world picture of Soviet actions. From the State Department's view, the idea of linkage hindered the arms limitation negotiations being conducted by the SALT team.

Nixon realized, however, that to secure such a pact, the United States had to deal from a position of strength. He had to make the Soviets eager to come to the bargaining table. Nixon the strategist wanted to have two cards to strengthen his hand: the first, an ABM (antiballistic missile), the defensive weapon to repel missile strikes; and second, rapprochement with mainland China, the Soviet's uneasy Marxist ally and also its historic adversary, with a population of almost a billion, at its southern border.

Almost all the leading experts, including State Department planners and academic specialists on Russia, recommended against these defense and foreign policy actions as "destabilizing"—in other words, menacing moves that would enhance

Kremlin paranoia and endanger the fragile prospects for negotiation. Even Kissinger, who agreed that passage of an ABM deployment by Congress would be a major bargaining chip, at first thought that gaining access to China would impair possibilities for détente.

Opposition to ABM grew to a crescendo as critics from a dovish press and Congress mounted their attack with two arguments that were illogical and inconsistent: first, that the building of such missiles was a belligerent and provocative act; and second, that the planned missile systems would not be technologically capable of repelling an attack.

Privately, Nixon argued that more important than the fact that the ABM *would* deflect such a missile strike was that it possibly *could*. An avid poker player during his navy days, Nixon told his friends that it was like an ace showing on the table in stud poker. The irony inherent in the left's attacks of the ABM was that Democrats opposed ABM because they believed it would *not* work, while the Russians opposed it because they believed it *would*. The Kremlin feared the prowess of American technology.

The Senate approval for the ABM passed by only one vote. Nixon and Chairman Mao Tse-tung achieved their history-making agreement in Beijing in February 1972, which resulted in the establishment of a U.S. mission in China. Now Nixon would be facing the Soviets with two strong cards. He had deployed an ABM system and combined it with a stepped-up MIRV (a system aimed at missile sites instead of cities). He now coupled the U.S. arms deployment with an approach to Moscow's potentially deadliest enemy, China. Nixon's critics called it "provocative." To Nixon, it was negotiating for peace from strength.

As the summit meeting in May 1972 neared, Nixon worried that the SALT negotiators, with each side fighting for a technological edge, would delay or stall an agreement on limitations on strategic arms. Without the negotiators' awareness, Nixon opened a private channel with Soviet ambassador Dobrynin to work out a general agreement.

Nixon then informed the SALT team in April of the agreed general lines he and Dobrynin had worked out. That was a signal to both bureaucracies, the U.S. State Department and the Soviets, to get down to business. (Nixon always believed that one by-product of a summit was to prod slow-moving bureaucrats.)

At the Moscow summit, Nixon and Party Secretary Brezhnev signed three important documents: the Antiballistic Missile Treaty; a preliminary accord on the limitation of Soviet arms; and a pact outlining the basic principles of U.S.–Soviet relations.

The results of the intense strategic preparations were the beginnings of détente. Nixon, who originally had doubts about summitry, would revise his opinion. He now advocated such meetings, provided they were not atmospheric but substantive. This could be achieved only by preliminary negotiations at all levels. The photo-op signing was then the icing on the cake. Nixon, by a careful orchestration, had achieved détente with the Soviet Union. Tensions between adversaries had been scaled down. The accommodation had been preceded by long negotiation made possible by intensive preparation.

Winston Churchill

In May 1953, at the Commonwealth Parliamentary Association meeting, Prime Minister Winston Churchill was in a receiving line when an eighteen-year-old Union scholar from America was introduced to him. His words of advice to me that day were: "Study history, study history—in history lie all the secrets of statecraft." Before America entered World War

II, Churchill studied the life of Franklin Roosevelt, reading speeches and articles both by and about him. If current events are present history, and history past politics, it can be said that Churchill, in his research on Roosevelt, was studying history.

Those studies intensified as he prepared for his first meeting with the American president in the summer of 1941. By that time, their exchanges of letters, which first began in 1937, had accelerated, along with frequent cables and telephone conversations with Roosevelt.

Yet Churchill wanted to take his personal measure of the man. Only in private meetings, without the attendance of aides, could Churchill match face to words and could he sense from Roosevelt's body language and voice the depth of his commitment to the war against Hitler.

Churchill's desire to meet Roosevelt was far more than curiosity. If an intimate rapport with Roosevelt was not established, any United States commitment to Britain was doubtful and the survival of Britain in danger. Churchill was in the role of a suitor: he had to woo Roosevelt. That meant he had to subdue his ego to engage Roosevelt's. His skills of oratory would, if anything, be counterproductive. He would not be speaking to the American people on a radio, but to its President in the intimacy of a private chat. He would have to resist his inclination to pontificate. In short, Churchill had to discipline himself to listen. To this end, he planned to emphasize that Roosevelt, like King George, was the head of state and that he, as head of government, ranked lower than the President, as head of state. To underscore that difference in rank, he asked King George for a message for him to deliver to President Roosevelt personally.

Churchill knew that in one-on-one selling, the opinions, ideas, and especially the very words of the persuadee make the difference. To that purpose, Churchill had his aides ransack the shelves in the library in the U.S. Embassy in Grosvenor Square. He read Roosevelt's speeches not just as president, but as far back as when he was state senator from New York. He searched through his recommendations as assistant secretary of the navy in World War I, looking for material that might parallel his own steps as first lord of the admiralty.

He studied not only Roosevelt's speeches as president that first addressed the dangers of fascism in Europe, but also his campaign speeches for vice president in 1920 on the need for a League of Nations. He was looking for Roosevelt's own words against American isolationism.

He even read articles about his hobbies of sailing and stamp collecting. Roosevelt, he learned, was not just "another former naval person" like Churchill, but an actual sailor who prided himself on his yachtsman skills, and that his early embrace of Woodrow Wilson's "self-determination" might have been shaped by his album of stamps that included the tiniest of nation-states.

In poring over the genealogy of the Roosevelts, he came across a common forebear, which he tucked away for future reference. Through his American mother's ancestors, Churchill also descended from a John Cooke in Massachusetts.

Churchill learned that Roosevelt was no Anglophile or imperialist like his distant cousin Theodore. To FDR, colonialism, in some respects, was hardly better than fascism. Because of this, alarm bells went off in Churchill's head when he received a telegram from the President in July 1941, outlining his draft of a statement that the leaders would issue on the shipboard meeting in August. It alluded to press speculation that Churchill was making private deals for postwar advantage with some exiled leaders of nations, such as Greece, who were living in London. Churchill thought the newspaper reports might have offended Roosevelt's strong belief in self-determination. If so, might Roosevelt use the meeting to criticize British colonialism in India and Africa?

Churchill reshaped the Anglo-American statement in grander and more general terms. His choice of the title of the agreement, "Atlantic Charter," had the echoes of the Magna Carta. He would hand his draft to Roosevelt personally on the ship and not send it to the White House where it could be screened and vetted by his staff.

Churchill knew it was imperative that if he could not actually break down the walls of this American fortress of neutrality—protected by its moat of thousands of miles of ocean—he must at least convey a perception that he had nudged America from its rigid policy of neutrality. The new mention of "Atlantic" in the charter was an attempt by Churchill to span the ocean dividing the two English-speaking powers.

After a train trip to the north of England in the cloak of night, Churchill secretly boarded the newest British battleship, the *Prince of Wales*, to head across the Atlantic.

Churchill planned even the smallest details for their shipboard meeting on the U.S. cruiser *Augusta* off the coast of Newfoundland. The former first lord of the admiralty personally supervised and reviewed the rehearsal of the Royal Navy's ceremonial reception of the American chief of state. He also arranged an Anglican shipboard service. He designated the reading of Psalm 35, which begins: "Plead my cause, O Lord, with them that strive with me; fight against them that fight against me." He chose the hymns "For Those in Peril on the Sea," a favorite of FDR and all sea lovers; the martial "Onward Christian Soldiers"; and the popular hymn "O God, Our Help in Ages Past." As Churchill knew, the Movietone newsreel clips of these two navies joining hands and singing hymns in unison would touch American hearts and make the idea of intervention more acceptable.

The spectacle of the two nations publicly worshiping together hinted at the private meetings of the two leaders, in which they exchanged military data and strategies. One result was that the United States agreed to send fleets to Iceland. When senators later told Roosevelt that this was a breach of the agreement that U.S. defense should include only the Western hemisphere, Roosevelt produced a specially created map showing Iceland in the Western hemisphere and not in Europe!

By dint of preparation, Churchill managed to give what was to be only a symbolic meeting the shadow of substance. Churchill wrote, "There is no substitute for the hard work of preparation." Nixon would have agreed.

Preparation, in diplomacy or business, might be described as strategic planning. Both Churchill and Nixon knew their objectives before they entered in a negotiation meeting, and they underwent the extensive preparation needed to accomplish those objectives. The more one knows about the other side's objectives and bargaining position, the stronger one's own position.

Most executives do not find *Alice in Wonderland* in the business school syllabus. Yet two lines there underscore the need for strategic planning. Alice asks the Red Queen for directions. The Queen answers, "That depends on where you want to go." And in another line, the Queen observes, "Now, *here*, you see, it takes all the running *you* can do, to keep in the same place. If you want to get somewhere else, you must run at least twice as fast as that!"

Strategic planning or preparation for negotiation, whether in the legal, business, or diplomatic world, is "running twice as fast." The lawyer works out the legal arguments that will be made against him. The businessman puts himself in the shoes of his contractual partner. The successful negotiator searches for any possible edge or advantage he can bring to the bargaining table. He does not dare to negotiate until he has done all that he can to prepare. The successful negotiator is the confident negotiator bolstered by advance knowledge and planning.

One of Nixon's foes in politics was Jesse Unruh, the one-time California Speaker of the House. Nixon once cited Jesse's famous maxim, "Money is the mother's milk of politics." "Well," said Nixon, "I would paraphrase that to say, 'Fact-finding is the mother's milk of negotiation.'"

II

NEVER BE BELLIGERENT,
BUT ALWAYS BE FIRM.

Nixon

Nixon's Second Commandment seems like an obvious truism. In the realm of personal conduct, its roots might be traced to a Biblical proverb Nixon's quiet-spoken Quaker mother could have recited to him. "A soft answer turneth away wrath." Yet in statecraft, it recalls one of the most quoted axioms in America—"Speak softly and carry a big stick; you will go far." Theodore Roosevelt first used it in a speech at the Minnesota state fair in 1901 to justify building a bigger navy in order to put teeth in the Monroe Doctrine.

Nixon's most publicized display of firmness instead of belligerence was in his cool counterattack to the blustering Khrushchev in the Kitchen Debate. Thirteen years later, Nixon had a confrontation with another Soviet chairman, which provides a better rationale of why Nixon yoked the two words in his warning. The avoidance of belligerency should not spell weakness. In fact, weakness often invites belligerency from exploitative aggressors, while firmness deters them.

Nixon, despite his Quaker mother, was not a pacifist in his religious beliefs or in his foreign policy principles.

In the spring of 1972, Nixon sensed a growing crack in the structure he had crafted for negotiation in the upcoming summit in May. The beginning of ABM deployment and the "triangulation" of the United States with the USSR and the People's Republic were the twin bulwarks of his strategy, but he worried that the sudden deterioration of the South Vietnamese army could weaken our negotiating posture, particularly if the Soviet's dependency, North Vietnam, overran our ally in the South.

Nixon knew he had to repair that position before the meeting in Moscow. After all, the real purpose of the summit was détente, and détente to Nixon meant "linkage." Linkage was the accountability of every Soviet move along the Cold War pressure points in the world. No area was more critical from the U.S. side than Vietnam.

Nixon was alarmed at the vision of Soviet tanks, with the North Vietnamese at the helm, rambling through the streets of Hue, as Soviet missiles, fired by the North Vietnamese, shelled Saigon. "If that happened, we couldn't have gone to the summit in Moscow," Nixon later said. "We wouldn't have been worth talking to, and the Soviets would have known it."

If the worsening of the Vietnamese situation was a widening crack, Nixon decided to cement it by mining Haiphong Harbor in order to prevent the shipment of Soviet arms and supplies.

When the President informed Senate leaders of his intentions, Mike Mansfield, the Democratic Senate majority leader, a mild-mannered Montanan, expostulated in anger, "How long ago were these orders issued?"

"Today," he was told.

The Democrats charged that this was a belligerent act

widening the war in Vietnam. Nixon answered that, on the contrary, mining the country was a "passive weapon."

Senate Democrats such as Frank Church predicted the mining would make the Soviets call off the summit. Senator George McGovern, then the likely Democratic presidential nominee, called it "a flirtation with World War III."

In Nixon's eyes, the mining action would not destroy but enhance the chances for détente at a summit. He deemed it not an act of aggression against the Soviet Union but a display of resolve and strength. Since Nixon took office in 1969, the Soviets had been pressing for a "summit conference," and Nixon was confident they would not call it off now. Their eagerness for our exports and our technology had not diminished.

Nixon believed that the only détente that would work was one that was self-enforcing—in other words, in the interests of both nations. A massive retreat of the South Vietnamese army would signal a weakness of the United States, which the Soviets would try to exploit. Such weakness might result not in negotiation but in dictation of terms by the Soviets. "Impotence," warned Nixon, "is not a positive force in diplomacy."

Just as Nixon predicted, the Soviets did not cancel the summit. At the Moscow meeting, Nixon was able to speak softly because the big sticks he was holding were already evident. In fact, in a press briefing before he left Moscow, he told reporters they would not hear "the overblown anti-Communist rhetoric" in which he admitted that he had often indulged in the past. Nixon had already made his point in mining Haiphong Harbor. Any rhetorical denunciation of Communists could make his resolve seem belligerent.

On the first meeting day on May 22, the negotiating styles of Nixon and Brezhnev were in sharp contrast. The experienced Nixon knew how to make his delivery forceful, even through an interpreter. He spoke slowly, in simple phrases, keeping eye contact with his listeners. After no longer than a minute, Nixon would stop, letting his interpreter begin his translation. During the translation, Nixon would smile, nod, and directly engage Brezhnev with eye contact to complement and enhance the translated version.

Brezhnev, on the other hand, spoke for at least three or four minutes and then appeared restless when his interpreter translated. He fidgeted and frequently glanced up at the ceiling. Yet Brezhnev, just like Nixon, had perfected the use of eyebrows to suggest doubt or bemusement at his counterpart's words. In these broadly attended sessions, Brezhnev managed to project an ursine amiability. He was neither strident nor rude. These businesslike conferences were punctuated by toasts of vodka, yet Nixon's experience with Khrushchev had taught him that the Russian teddy bear could turn, in a flash, into a grizzly.

On May 24, Nixon, along with Kissinger and his aide Winston Lord, was invited to Brezhnev's dacha in a forest outside Moscow. Following a late-afternoon boat ride down the Moscow River, the two sides gathered in a small room dominated by a long table. Brezhnev, Kosygin, Podgorny, and an interpreter sat on one side, and Nixon, Kissinger, Lord, and their interpreter sat on the other.

Without any opening amenities, Brezhnev suddenly erupted with vituperation. "The mining," roared the Soviet chairman, "was barbaric, exceeding that of the Nazis." He concluded his tirade with reference to their own missile capability.

Nixon answered coolly, "Is that a threat?"

Brezhnev resumed his denunciation. Pounding the table, he warned of serious consequences if any Soviet sailors were lost by the mining of the harbor.

Nixon again responded, "Is that a threat?"

Another savage blast by Brezhnev was again followed by Nixon's soft, measured words, "Are we threatening here?" Nixon's cool replies eventually defused the tense atmosphere.

But later Brezhnev again resumed his onslaught. Nixon deflected the outburst by repeating the same words: "Is that a threat?"

Nixon understood that Brezhnev had lost face by not calling off the summit after the Haiphong Harbor mining, and he was determined to remain stolid and impassive in the face of Soviet ranting. He recognized that such belligerence is bluster, a sign of weakness, not confidence. When the meeting was over and the dacha table had ended, they adjourned upstairs to a dining room where the Russians quickly turned jovial. With the Soviets it was often bombast followed by laughter; saber rattling giving way to smiles; and then the hard work of negotiation succeeded by hard drinking. (At one point Nixon joked to Brezhnev that he was trying to get Kissinger drunk, and Brezhnev played along with the gag by constantly pouring vodka into the National Security Council head's glass.)

Nixon never lost sight of his objective of détente, which would be symbolized by a signed agreement on the limitation of arms. What was not recorded on paper was an understanding that the Soviets would signal to its ally North Vietnam its nonenthusiasm for a continuance of the conflict. In other words, the Soviets began to encourage in the North Vietnamese a real commitment to peace negotiations. Nixon knew the difference between being firm and belligerent, and in his negotiation he manifested resolve and avoided empty threats of retaliation.

General Santa Anna

G eneral Santa Anna is to many a dim figure in American history, but he remains a legend in Texas and California. For children growing up in those former Spanish colonies, the Mexican War is more important than the Civil War, and General Santa Anna is more reviled than General Sherman in the South. Today, many historians blame the war on an imperialist America intoxicated by dreams of "manifest destiny." The United States did acquire the northern provinces of Mexico as a result of the war, but it was Santa Anna's reckless belligerence that fueled the American hostility against Mexico and provoked the demands for the confrontation.

Antonio López de Santa Anna was born in 1794 in the province of Veracruz in eastern New Spain (now Mexico). He later took the name of Santa Anna (St. Anne), perhaps because López was so common a surname in New Spain. Though there was no Indian blood in his ancestry, Santa Anna was still a "Creole"—which meant he was born in Mexico. Only those born in Spain were deemed true Spaniards and qualified as aristocrats; the Creoles were a step down in the social pecking order. This might explain why Santa Anna became almost a caricature of the Spanish caballero. He chose the aristocratic calling of the military and comported himself as a macho officer, notoriously sensitive to slights to his dignity and honor.

In 1810, at age sixteen, Santa Anna falsified his age to enter the Spanish army as a cadet, where he took the first opportunity to join the cavalry division, traditionally favored by the better born. His early idol was Napoleon, and he even arranged his hair from back to front and bought a white charger to resemble that of his hero. An early portrait of the young officer shows him tucking his right hand into his waistcoat in the signature fashion of Napoleon.

Three years later, as a young officer, Santa Anna took part in the ousting of a motley crew of American adventurers and Indians who were making settlements near Laredo. In addition to the 850 Americans killed in battle, 112 were taken prisoner, and subsequently shot. Then the regiment marched to San Antonio, where, after an easy military victory, they killed 250 captured rebels by firing squad. Captain Santa Anna learned two bad lessons from this experience: that the Americans were poor fighters and that the way to handle them was through terrorization.

On February 21, 1821, Colonel Agustín de Iturbide, formerly a royalist officer of New Spain, made his famous Pronouncement of Iguala, in which he formed the Army of the Three Guarantees. The pledges included the absolute independence of Mexico, the union of Europeans and Mexicans in this new nation, and the preservation of the Catholic faith, with no toleration for other religions. Santa Anna, now lieutenant colonel—after a decade of service as a loyal royalist officer suppressing local uprisings against the government— was summoned to quell an insurrection at Orizaba. Santa Anna, the Spanish officer, defected to the insurgency forces when rebel General Herrera offered to make him colonel and governor of the province of Veracruz.

In Mexico City, the victorious Iturbide routed the colonial government and proclaimed himself the new emperor of Mexico. For some years, Santa Anna lent himself to the intrigues to overthrow Iturbide. In 1823, Iturbide was finally dethroned, and a republic was formed. Since Santa Anna was the most prominent general of the opposition who had not been disgraced or totally discredited, he was elected president in 1833.

With his presidential sash, the thirty-eight-year-old President Santa Anna manifested an imposing presence: tall, slender, with a smallish Grecian nose, black darting eyes, and pale skin.

Texas was the new government's most troublesome province. Ever since the American colonies had won their independence, Spain—and then Mexico—had difficulties with this northernmost region.

To populate the sparse and arid terrain, Spain, in the early nineteenth century, had accepted Moses Austin's offer to bring in American settlers. Mexico continued the practice with its colonization law of 1830. The almost one-thousand-mile distance from San Antonio to Mexico City and the differences in religion and race made a clash between the settlers and the Mexican government inevitable. The Anglo-American Protestants in Texas were naturally hostile to the "centralistas" in Mexico, preferring the looser autonomy of federalism.

The American former governor of Tennessee, Sam Houston, was looked upon as the leader of the American settlers. The "father of Texas," on March 2, 1836, declared the independence of Texas, asserting that "General Santa Anna and other chieftains had by force overthrown the federal constitution." In this uprising against the dictatorial regime in Mexico City, the Americans had the support of like-minded Mexican "federalistas," who bridled at the oppressive interference of the capital city government.

Mexican president Santa Anna quickly mobilized an army of six thousand soldiers. The threatening circumstances brought to the fore the best and worst of Santa Anna. As an orator, his perfervid declarations would arouse and inspire the campesinos to leave their families in the quest for glory on this "holy crusade in behalf of the Blessed Virgin" to reclaim the sacred soil of Mexico from "Protestants who defile her name." As a special incentive to the mestizo peasants, Santa Anna, again inspired by Napoleon, created a special decoration, the Legion of Honor.

Unfortunately, like so many demagogues, Santa Anna tended to believe his own cant. He convinced himself that the Americans in the Texas province were ragtag rebels, with neither the honor nor the valor that was the code of every Mexican.

Santa Anna's assault on the Alamo on the outskirts of San Antonio lasted for thirteen days. The Texans, under the command of Colonel William Travis, took refuge in an old Franciscan mission. On Sunday morning, March 6, 1836, Santa Anna's army killed 183 Texans. The general justified the near-complete extermination with a document he had issued three months earlier, stating that "all foreigners who landed anywhere in the republic for purposes of taking up arms—shall be treated and punished as pirates."

After the Alamo victory, the Mexican troops marched to Goliad on the coast. James Fannin, who captained some volunteers under the new Lone Star flag of the Republic of Texas, took one look at the overwhelming superiority of the Mexican army and surrendered. On March 26, orders came from General Santa Anna to "execute all prisoners." Amazingly, Santa Anna thought he was acting as a man of honor, but to Texans, he was a man of horror who personified a savage Mexican government. Santa Anna's policy was more than mere belligerency. It was naked brutality. Rumors—later substantiated—claimed that Santa Anna, in his home in Veracruz, often tortured dogs to test their endurance for pain. To the American settlers in Texas, for whom the rifle and dog were extensions of themselves, this was further proof of his inhuman cruelty. The Santa Anna atrocities steeled General Sam Houston's resolve. He recruited all the forces he could muster to defeat the Mexican president.

In San Jacinto, a small Texas town, on a river by that name, the general was resting his troops for a final march to the region of the province that bordered the United States. The Houston forces sneaked past the sentries of the Mexican encampment at night and launched their raid, shouting "Remember the Alamo," "Remember Goliad," and "Death to Santa Anna." In a vain effort to stir his troops, Santa Anna cried out, "The enemy is upon us." On April 21 (now a holiday in Texas, San Jacinto Day), the Mexican army was completely annihilated—one half killed and the rest wounded and captured. Even Santa Anna's horse was shot out from under him. Santa Anna, disguising himself, managed to escape but was captured a few days later.

Santa Anna was taken to General Houston's headquarters at San Jacinto, and there he surrendered and signed two treaties: one for the evacuation of Mexican troops and the other for the restoration of Texas's property. He also made a secret agreement with Houston to recommend independence for Texas to the Mexican government. He probably would have agreed to anything to get out of Texas alive. At Velasco, where he was about to set sail for Veracruz, a volunteer force of Americans from New Orleans stormed his ship. They would have killed Santa Anna if not for the intervention of Stephen Austin (the son of Moses Austin and civilian leader of the American settlers), who put him under house arrest and suggested he write President Andrew Jackson to ensure his safe passage home.

The Mexican government negotiated for his release, but the loser would not be welcomed back to Mexico City. Santa Anna's reputation for bravado, when mixed with the debacle of defeat, cost him the presidency. He was ousted upon his return.

Despite his dismissal, the career of General Santa Anna did not end in 1836. In a sense, he was a forerunner of the many caudillos or presidential strongmen who have played dominant roles in Latin American history. In this century, we have seen Perón, Trujillo, Batista, and, most recently, Castro.

Five times the charisma and oratory of Santa Anna would return him to the presidency. Each time, his corruption and deceit would prove his demise. His dealings with the Americans in the Mexican War a decade later are a testament to his duplicity. In 1845, the self-styled general personally sent letters to President Polk, recommending that America send an army to the Rio Grande and a naval force to Veracruz demanding payments from the Mexican government, while at the same time, he was publicly denouncing U.S. imperialism. In other words, he wanted a war, which he hoped would force the Mexican government to call on his military leadership.

If Santa Anna had spared the captured American soldiers at the Alamo and Goliad and treated them with even minimal regard and respect, the vastly outnumbered Texans might have been impelled to lay down their arms and come to terms with the Mexican government and accept some federal arrangement of autonomy. The heedless butchery by Santa Anna left Texans with no choice but to fight for their lives.

In his book *Negotiating Game,* Chester Karrass notes that "people react violently to being assaulted but will be responsive when claims are rational."

Firmness is a necessary requisite in dealing with adversaries, as Nixon's strategy leading up to the 1972 summit illustrates, but needless belligerency, gratuitous insults, and provocative actions disrupt communications and destroy any chance for negotiating success.

In 1990, Nixon viewed, with some of his family, Kenneth Branagh's movie *Henry V,* based on Shakespeare's play. When Henry, still in his twenties, assumed the English throne, he sent a note to France signaling his intention to negotiate peacefully their differences. The response of the Dauphin, son

III

ALWAYS REMEMBER THAT COVENANTS SHOULD BE OPENLY AGREED TO BUT PRIVATELY NEGOTIATED.

Nixon

In 1988, I asked Nixon, "Mr. President, was winning the pact with Red China like wooing a nun?"

The former president nodded and started to laugh, but his political reflexes caused a belated frown. He had too many good Catholic friends.

Presidential secrecy in foreign affairs had always rankled Congress. In the fifties, Republicans, who thought that the Yalta meeting in 1945 of Roosevelt and Stalin was a cave-in to Stalin's demands in Poland and Eastern Europe, pushed for the Bricker Amendment to constrain the President's hand in foreign dealings. In the seventies, Democrats in Congress accused Nixon of "wheeling and dealing" with little input from Congress. The fact is that Nixon could never have pulled off the Beijing meeting of 1972 without secrecy.

Yet Americans, because of their attachment to direct democracy, are suspicious of secret diplomacy. The populist sentiments of Americans associate striped-pants diplomats with monarchies. In World War I, Woodrow Wilson tapped this distrust of the Old World by pledging "open covenants" in Versailles.

It is not an accident that Nixon used the words *covenants* and *openly* in this Third Commandment. In Nixon's formative years, many in his California Quaker community believed that the idealism of Wilson was crushed by the aggressiveness of political manipulators like British prime minister David Lloyd George and French premier Georges Clemenceau.

But if he had not added "but privately negotiated," this commandment would be no more instructive than "honor thy mother" or "love the flag." In "privately negotiated," Nixon was not only offering advice but defending his negotiating style, exemplified in his dealings with the People's Republic of China.

Nixon had to cloak his overtures under a blanket of secrecy. The prying eyes of his own State Department were hardest to shield. The State Department was rigid in its analysis of the People's Republic, insisting that only if the United States ended the Vietnam War and conceded Taiwan to the People's Republic could access to China be established. Even if President Nixon had tried to involve the State Department in the early maneuvering, he would have met with resistance. The planners at State would no doubt have considered the overtures to China as threatening their SALT disarmament negotiations with the USSR.

Of course, if the State Department was brought into the maneuvering, the Soviets would have found out about Nixon's move toward its massive neighbor on its southern flank. In State's massive bureaucracy located in Foggy Bottom—an allusion to this former swampland that oozed a miasma of mists—no "top secret" classification can ever dike the oozing leakage. Overreaction by the Soviets was a real risk. But as it happened, Nixon was able to woo the Soviets into a false sense of complacency. As hints about Nixon's dealings with China began to surface, Nixon told Soviet ambassador Dobrynin that whatever he might hear, the Soviets should realize that Nixon was solely concerned about China and Chinese affairs and not with influencing the Soviet Union through China.

In addition, if Nixon had consulted with Congress, he would have antagonized elements in his own Republican Party who were staunch supporters of the United States–Taiwan alliance. When President Nixon did announce his receipt of an invitation from the People's Republic, he maintained that the opening to China did not mean a lessening of U.S. commitment to Taiwan. In this case, he was being a bit economical with the truth. True, the defense treaty with Taiwan was not abrogated, but the opening to the People's Republic was, in diplomatic psychology, a loss of face for the Nationalist Chinese Republic.

Finally, not the least determined to maintain secrecy were Chou En-lai and Mao Tse-tung. In 1972, the purges of the Cultural Revolution were not over. The news that their leaders would be communicating or meeting with "the running dog capitalists" infuriated many Chinese Communist Party leaders. For pragmatic reasons of geopolitical self-interest, Mao and Chou were receptive to U.S. overtures, but it would have been a difficult sell to the Marxist zealots of the party. Later, Chou En-lai would reveal to Henry Kissinger his unease about the forces that the Cultural Revolution had unleashed.

It has been said that in the bridge to mainland China, Nixon was the architect and Kissinger the engineer. If so, Kissinger was not originally happy with the plans and specifications. It was Nixon, not Kissinger, who conceived of the approach, as his 1967 article "What After Viet Nam?" attests.

Kissinger's interest and expertise in China was only marginally greater than his knowledge of the moon. Unlike

Nixon, who grew up on the shores of the Pacific, Kissinger had been born in Europe. His native language being German, Kissinger typically chose Bismarck and Metternich as subjects for his academic study. Both the Prussian and the Austrian practiced secret diplomacy to attain their Realpolitik objectives.

If China policy held little interest for Kissinger, his fascination for the craft and guile of Bismarck and Metternich would serve him well in the nuanced negotiation with the Chinese. Kissinger was contemptuous of the Sunday school idealism of Wilsonian diplomacy, considering it not just unproductive but counterproductive.

Still, in 1969, Kissinger's dominant priority was Soviet relations and the politics of missile weaponry. Any move toward China might threaten the objective of détente. As Kissinger told his deputy, Al Haig, "This crazy guy really does want to normalize our relations in China." The word "triangularization" may have been first coined by Kissinger in backgrounders to newsmen to explain the inclusion of China in the U.S. policy to accomplish détente with the Soviet Union, but the concept was Nixon's.

Although Nixon would later bar the State Department from involvement in the China approach, he did allow State, in January 1970, to organize the first meeting between the new administration and the People's Republic of China, which took place at the Chinese Embassy in Warsaw. This was the 135th such meeting since 1962, and all had been futile. The issue of Taiwan was the sticking point each time. Nixon instructed our ambassador, over the protests of the State Department, to say that we would consider sending a representative to Beijing or receiving one in Washington for direct discussions.

In a note that was conciliatory, the Chinese did not

respond to the initiative but did not reject it. Due to the State Department's coolness to the idea, Nixon had to develop a back channel with the Chinese. Nixon embarked on a diplomatic minuet involving at least three foreign governments, including France, Pakistan, and Romania.

Nixon orchestrated all the early maneuvers himself without Kissinger, in part because the strategy involved partners like de Gaulle of France, Ceauşescu of Romania, and Yahya Khan of Pakistan, whom he alone could approach.* These heads of government then made oblique references to Chinese ambassadors in their capital city about a new attitude in Washington.

To give some substance to the rumors being floated by these leaders, Nixon, in April 1970, freed for export to China goods manufactured in other countries with American components. In July, China responded by releasing Bishop Walsh, a Catholic priest imprisoned in China. In July, Nixon lifted restrictions that for twenty years had prohibited American oil companies abroad from refueling ships bound for China.

A month later, Nixon had Kissinger add this pregnant line in an address to Midwestern newspaper editors: "The deepest rivalry which may exist in the world today . . . is that between the Soviet Union and China."

In October, Mao Tse-tung and Chou En-lai answered in such a subtle signal that it was almost not caught: the American writer Edgar Snow—an old friend of the Chinese Com-

---

* There is a Chinese folk saying, "Only an elephant can talk to an elephant." Heads of governments, like many CEOs, do not fully trust even their own top deputies. As for aides of competing or rival leaders, they are wary of the spin or twist put upon their remarks. The aide's first priority is survival. C.Y.A. (cover your ass) is the cardinal precept of bureaucrats, which makes the handling of their instructions formulaic, rigid, and unimaginative.

munists—stood beside Mao to be photographed in the October 1 national holiday parade.

Nixon, in a long *Time* magazine interview, made the off-hand remark, "If there is anything I want to do before I die, it is to go to China." A few days later, in a state visit of President Yahya Khan of Pakistan, a close ally of China, Nixon indicated willingness to send a high-level secret emissary to China.

Then, when Romanian President Ceauşescu came to Washington on October 26, Nixon, in a toast at a state dinner, mentioned the good relations Romania had with, among others, "the People's Republic of China." It was the first use of China's official name by a U.S. president.

In December, the Pakistani ambassador personally delivered a letter to President Nixon from Chou En-lai stating that China would be receptive to a visit by a special envoy.

Nixon reacted in the spring of 1971 by lifting all restrictions on the use of U.S. passports for travel to China. If this exchange of volleys suggested a game of Ping-Pong, it was fitting that the Chinese Reds first surfaced publicly by inviting the U.S. Ping-Pong team, which was competing in Japan on April 4, to come to Beijing on April 14. Chou received the delegation of American table tennis players in the Great Hall of the People. Few Western diplomats stationed in Beijing had ever been accorded this honor.

Chou En-lai greeted them saying, "You have opened a new page in the relations of the Chinese and American people. I am confident that this beginning again of our friendship will certainly meet with majority support of two peoples." When the stunned athletes did not respond, the Premier pushed the subject. "Don't you agree with me?" The Americans burst into applause and promptly asked the Chinese team to tour the United States.

Chou En-lai chose the athletes as the recipients of his message because they had no political coloration and thus would trigger negative spins in neither of the two countries. Still, by this ceremonial reception, the Chinese had given a public answer to the calibrated series of hints, gestures, and signals by Nixon.

The possibility of normalization was no longer confined to back channels. On December 16, 1970, Nixon sent a message to China indicating his willingness to send an envoy. Time stood still. Months passed. Nixon fretted that his initiative may have failed.

In April 1971, the Pakistan ambassador relayed Chou En-lai's response: "The Chinese government reaffirms its willingness to receive publicly in Beijing a special envoy of the President."

Nixon did not, of course, make public the invitation, but he did, through the back channel of Pakistan, inquire about possible dates. At a state dinner on June 2 for the President of Nicaragua, Kissinger asked a military aide to see the President for a moment. Nixon read the message delivered by Kissinger, which contained the words "a date between June 15 and June 20 for his arrival in China" and that "he [the special envoy, i.e., Kissinger] may fly direct from Islamabad (Pakistan) to a Chinese airport not open to the public." Because of time constraints, Nixon and Kissinger suggested an alternative date of arriving in China on July 9 and leaving July 11.

On June 30, Press Secretary Ron Ziegler announced that Nixon was sending Kissinger on a fact-finding mission to Vietnam and then to Paris, and on the way, to confer with officials in Thailand, India, and Pakistan.*

*Kissinger at first refused to go. He thought the secret dealings would destroy the chances of détente with the Soviet Union, which was his prime objective. He went to the home of his German mentor, Fritz Kramer, and wept that his career would be destroyed. Kramer told him, "With two enemies, you help the lesser one." When Kissinger returned to Nixon and revealed his misgivings, Nixon suggested his replacement by Secretary of State William Rogers. Kissinger agreed to go.

Henry Kissinger left on July 1. He would arrive in Pakistan on July 8. At a state dinner in his honor, Kissinger complained of stomach pains. Following his script, the President of Pakistan suggested that he be taken to a presidential guest house in the halls outside Islamabad.

At 3:30 A.M. on July 9, Kissinger, masked in a hat and sunglasses, was taken by limousine to a military airport where he boarded a plane to China. He landed at a military airport in the outskirts of Beijing at 12:15 Friday, July 9 (China time). At 4:30 Chou En-lai visited the guest house where Kissinger and his party were staying. The meeting the next day would culminate in an invitation to President Nixon to visit China in January 1972. The announcement by President Nixon on July 15 that he had accepted the Chinese premier's invitation to visit China shook the world. In London, former British prime minister Harold Macmillan recalled the historic comment of the nineteenth-century statesman George Canning, "I have brought the New World into existence to redress the balance of the Old," and added that Nixon had reversed the British prime minister. "He's brought the oldest civilization in the world back into the game to redress the new Russian empire."

If secrecy is a cloak for corrupt deals and international chicanery, it is a sin in democracy. Yet, as Nixon proved, in camera proceedings can be a catalyst for diplomatic breakthroughs in cases when the glare of the press would have scorched the possible flowering of any settlement. The diplomatic triumph of the century would never have occurred in the white heat of publicity.

Prince Metternich

Nixon first heard the name of Metternich in 1930 in his European history class at Whittier High School. Later, as the top honors history major at Whittier College, he would write a paper on the Congress of Vienna.

Metternich, lover of diplomatic intrigue and fashionable courtesans, was no hero to the young and idealistic Nixon. But later, in the White House around 1970, Nixon came to appreciate the talents of this negotiating craftsman when he chose for his bedtime reading de Sauvigny's biography of Metternich.

Several of Metternich's own "commandments of statecraft" must have appealed to the President, who was laying plans for negotiations with the Soviet Union, China, and North Vietnam. These maxims, quoted from Metternich's letters, appear in de Sauvigny's biography:

- It seems to me that in politics, as in war, an offensive or defensive plan must be adapted to the characteristics of the adversary.
- It often happens that it is extremely difficult to disentangle the true from the false, but a man has one guide that rarely lets him down; namely, the calculation of interest.
- Sleep on questions that are extremely difficult . . . to wait and not to judge in a hurry.
- Tact goes farther in business than intelligence.
- The more diffusely and less accurately questions are framed—the harder it is to resolve an issue.

- Failure to honor engagements entered into is the biggest mistake a government can make.
- To try to put oneself against the natural order of things is folly.

Klemens Wenzel Nepomuk Lothar von Metternich was born in a Rhineland country manor in Kohberg in 1773. Because of its proximity to the French border, he grew up speaking both French and German. His fluency in French may have destined him for a career in diplomacy. The son of an imperial count, he had the advantage of having a French tutor who exposed him to the theories of the Enlightenment.

At the age of twenty-four, after studying at the universities of both Strasbourg and Mainz, Metternich served as the diplomatic secretary to his father, who was the Westphalian ambassador to the Holy Roman Empire. Then in 1801, at age twenty-seven, he secured his first post as the Emperor's envoy to Saxony in Dresden.

Biographer Alan Palmer notes that the Dresden appointment was a turning point in his life. "He now saw the problems of the continent less as a Rhinelander and far more as a European." The rise of Napoleon and the advance of his armies across Europe strengthened this Continental outlook.

In August 1806, Metternich went to Paris as ambassador, where he would have his first face-to-face confrontation with Napoleon. Intellectually, Metternich came to respect the mind of the Emperor, who was four years his senior. But politically and socially, he disdained this Corsican upstart. He considered him a child of the French Revolution and a brattish one at that.

Austria, however, needed breathing space after its disastrous defeat by Napoleon at Austerlitz in December 1805. Metternich wanted time to repair Austria's broken army and replenish the treasury, and he purchased it by arranging a marriage of Austria's Princess Marie Louise to the childless Napoleon, who was desperate for a royal heir. Pragmatism prevailed over Metternich's personal distaste for the "Corsican corporal."

Napoleon's dominance of Europe lasted until October 1813, when his armies were defeated at Leipzig. The following March, Allied armies marched through Paris. Napoleon abdicated and sailed to Elba in exile.

Napoleon was gone, but the wreckage of Europe was left behind him. Thrones had been toppled, principalities eliminated, and borders revised. A new code of laws had replaced old systems of justice.

Metternich was perhaps the first Europeanist, and he shuddered at the havoc Napoleon had inflicted upon the continent. The accepted wisdom is that the Austrian prince wanted a restoration of the Old Order (the ancien régime). Actually, his first priority was peace.

Metternich was not like Woodrow Wilson, who would try to impose his vision upon others. He had no map in his head of what Europe should ideally look like. Neither was he a romanticist about royalty. He was not one to sacrifice a career or country for an abstraction. He was a realist. He had one objective, and that was order—not necessarily the "Old Order"—but a stability in Europe that could bring a lasting peace. Peace was Metternich's destination, and he would arrive there on a carriage called practicality and a horse named flexibility.

As soon as the Battle of Leipzig was won, Metternich had proposed Vienna as a meeting place for sovereigns. After the signing of the Peace of Paris in March, "all persons engaged on either side in the present war" were asked to send delegates to Vienna.

Never in history had there been such an international assembly as the Congress of Vienna. The city was the perfect venue for Metternich's purposes. It offered settings for both stately pomp and secret planning. The statesmen could meet formally in vast halls against a backdrop of marble and malachite, with twisted columns rising to some apocalyptic vision on a painted dome, or they could retire to the salons of the great town houses, where massive wooden gates shut out the world.

From every corner of Europe, a hundred thousand visitors poured into Vienna—half again as many as the city's total population. No fewer than 215 heads of princely families arrived with their retinues of servants, as well as their ministers, statesmen, diplomats, aides, and secretaries.

Metternich called the Congress a "festival for peace," and he appointed a festival committee to arrange gala receptions and entertainments. The Emperor and Empress of Austria daily toasted their royal visitors at social functions. But it was Metternich's plan to distract and dazzle these royal nabobs with dances, balls, concerts, operas, and theatricals, as well as exhibitions of the famous Lipizzaner horses of the Spanish Riding School. (One ball opened with an all-Beethoven concert. The composer himself appeared and conducted the Seventh Symphony for the first time.) Pomp would take the place of power for the lesser ducal delegates. After many months of these glittering activities, Prince Charles de Ligne commented, *"Le Congrès ne marche pas; il danse."* (The Congress does not progress; it dances.) Czar Alexander I of Russia would say, "You must give Metternich credit for this. He is a marvelous master of ceremonies."

Along with the Czar, the major monarchs attending were Emperor Francis I of Austria and King Frederick William of Prussia. On display in the British Museum is a print by a nineteenth-century French artist depicting those who would be the real power brokers at the Congress. Besides Metternich were the Prussian chancellor, Prince Karl August von Hardenberg;

the Russian foreign minister, Count Karl Robert Nesselrode; the French foreign minister, Prince Charles-Maurice de Talleyrand, who deserted Napoleon in his final months; and representing Britain, the Duke of Wellington, the recently victorious general and now ambassador to France, and Viscount Castlereagh, the British foreign secretary.

Metternich did not wish to meet these "movers and shakers" of the boundaries and the empires of Europe around a green baize conference table. Rather, he negotiated with each of them in clandestine conversations. He knew peace could not be brokered in any group discussion. He was aware of the "wish list" of all the big winners in the war against Napoleon, and he knew which demands, if not satisfied, could plunge Europe back into war.

Czar Alexander I of Russia presented the most difficult case. He wanted Poland as a satellite kingdom. The Czar, who had marched with his armies into Paris for the defeat of Napoleon, believed Poland was his, both by divine right and military spoils. Napoleon once said of him, "No one could exceed him in intelligence, but there was one piece missing in his head." Perhaps Napoleon was referring to the Czar's messianic belief that God had appointed him the savior of the Slavs.

King Frederick William of Prussia coveted the German kingdom of Saxony, whose king had unfortunately sided with Napoleon in the recent war. Castlereagh, the British foreign secretary, supported the demands of Prussia. Britain thought every enlargement of czarist Russia a peril and that any gain by Prussia was an enhancement of peace. Finally, Prince Talleyrand, who represented the defeated France, was in no position to demand anything. Officially, he represented Louis XVIII of France, whom the victorious powers had put back on the French throne because they could not come up with a better alternative.

JAMES C. HUMES

In actuality, the wily Talleyrand assumed the political voice of France when he abandoned Napoleon. It is a tribute to his skills of statecraft that Talleyrand came to the Congress as an outsider, but left as an insider. The Big Four—Metternich, Hardenberg, Nesselrode, and Castlereagh—expanded into the Big Five. Although Talleyrand told the other four that he was the only one who came with no demands, he had two objectives: a Bourbon monarchy returned to rule Spain and the Kingdom of the Two Sicilies and the art that Napoleon had looted in his conquests to remain in the Louvre.

Even before the royal delegates assembled, Metternich announced that Austria was abandoning its claim upon the Netherlands, the last rich remnant of the old inheritance of the Hapsburgs. This was his signal to the other royal principals not to be set in their ways. To forge peace, some flexibility was essential.

Metternich's gift, however, was not without guile. Austria had reason to yield claims to noncontiguous territory and aim at consolidation. Metternich believed that in the future, his nation should look to the south, not the north. Furthermore, by returning the Flemish and Walloon provinces, Metternich compensated Holland for its loss of the Cape in South Africa to the British. Britain now owed Metternich a chit.

Peace was the picture he was striving for, but the pieces of the puzzle—scattered to the winds in the wake of Napoleon—had to be put back in such a way as not to offend the dominant powers. He envisioned two nations anchoring central Europe. Prussia would play a leadership role amongst the many Germanic states in the north, while Austria would dominate the Slav peoples and the Italian states of Venetia and Lombardy to the south.

Britain agreed to accept such a settlement if Russia was deterred from annexing Poland. France was amenable if Prussia was not permitted to grab Saxony. The hard sell would be with Czar Alexander I of Russia and King Frederick William of Prussia.

For his one-on-one private meetings with the two diplomats representing those states, Nesselrode of Russia and von Hardenberg of Prussia, Metternich relied on his private intelligence network.

Metternich once wrote, "A minister is never far from going astray when he allows himself to form a judgment based on the information of one isolated subordinate." The couriers of the information he required were courtesans. Metternich's mistress, Wilhemine, the Duchess of Sagan, had been a former lover of Czar Alexander I. Wilhemine not only was still on intimate terms with the Czar but knew key members of his entourage, with whom she could converse in French and German as well as Russian.

During the Congress, she maintained an ongoing salon where a favored guest was Wilhelm von Humboldt, the Prussian foreign secretary and the top lieutenant of Chancellor Hardenberg. Wilhemine's younger sister, Princess Dorothea, was a niece-in-law of Talleyrand. During the Congress, she acted as hostess for the French diplomat and was instrumental in securing Talleyrand as a partner in Metternich's plans.

Witty and elegant, Wilhemine played on Alexander's continuing attachment to her and became the intermediary between Metternich and the Czar. Born in Silesia, an eastern German state, she was related distantly to the Czar on her mother's side. Her sister was not quite as beautiful but was twelve years younger. In the morning, Dorothea went over the letters and messages to Talleyrand and helped draft the replies. In the evening, she either was a hostess for a private party or the guest at someone else's fete, where her jewels, youth, and intelligence made her a favorite dancing and dinner partner. Because Talleyrand was most suspicious of Prussia, she made befriending of the Prussian diplomatic entourage a priority. She shared the intelligence she gleaned both with Talleyrand and her sister, Wilhemine, the mistress of Metternich.

Flirtation and feminine favors constituted Metternich's intelligence network. In the late morning, he and Wilhemine would receive reports through the bedrooms as well as the salons. Metternich orchestrated a broad outline of agreement upon the new configuration of Europe. Of the principals, only Castlereagh kept a distance from the amorous intrigues. But if he disapproved of the Continental morals of the royals, he approved of the ends that the means afforded.

The Czar did not take over all of Poland. Austria got the port of Cracow and Prussia received the Polish city of Thurn, with the Warta River as a defensible frontier. That satisfied England, because it gave Prussia a river border to defend against czarist troops if they marched west through Poland.

Prussia did not annex all of Saxony. King Frederick, over King Frederick William's objections, was returned his throne, but only half his country, which included Leipzig and Dresden. The other half of the country, bordering the Elbe, went to Prussia.

The final settlement also echoed Talleyrand's wish that the Bourbons be returned to the thrones of Spain and the Kingdom of Sicily and Naples. The northern part of Italy, Venetia and Lombardy, was restored to the Austrian empire.

The final agreement reflected Metternich's hardheaded assessment of what was needed to prevent war. He envisioned a united Europe whose five great powers—Austria, Prussia, Russia, France, and Britain—lived in constructive harmony.

The notion that such a peace accord could have been worked out by all the delegates in public discussion in some concert of nations at Schönbrunn Palace is fantasy. Nor is it likely that such an agreement could have been reached by the four or five principals in a group format similar to the Big

Three in Yalta in 1945. Metternich practiced a secret diplomacy. Some have called it salon scheming.

Today, democrats would bridle at the secrecy of deal making in private salons, and moralists would be sickened at the use of bedchambers for negotiation. Realists, however, might recognize, as Nixon and Kissinger did, that the subterranean intrigues of Vienna produced a much longer peace than the idealism gone awry at Versailles a century later.

These same principles could just as easily apply to the takeover of a company, as of a country. In a business setting, as in diplomacy, a large forum—in which all the parties air their views—is often counterproductive, as each side vies against the others to put on a better show for the interests they represent.

In contrast, off-the-record talks provide a more intimate setting, which encourages parties to take risks that, if they were to become public, would result in loss of face. Public display has its place, both in business and politics, but the purpose should be symbolic, not substantive. In 1972, Nixon, in the Beijing airport, extended his hand to Chou En-lai, whose outstretched hand had been spurned by Secretary of State John Foster Dulles in 1954. It costs nothing to give all due deference to the negotiating adversary, and it pays dividends. Some CEOs play one-upmanship by staging higher seats for themselves or uncomfortable chairs for the competition. That executive is parading his insecurity, not his strength.

Business leaders can negotiate by press release or news conferences, but such public tactics tend to harden the other side's positions. Substantive progress in reaching an accommodation is done in private. Successful diplomatic or business negotiators resist the temptation to grandstand or make public demands that can be interpreted as threats.

IV

NEVER SEEK PUBLICITY
THAT WOULD DESTROY THE
ABILITY TO GET RESULTS.

Nixon

The Fourth Commandment is as old as the Greek concept of hubris. King Solomon was the author of a similar maxim in Proverbs: "Pride goeth before destruction." In English folklore, it was not so much a matter of religion as superstition. "Don't count your chickens before they're hatched" was a warning against speaking out too soon.

In government, Nixon knew that advance publicity could be a double-edged sword. On the one hand, the leader is tempted to announce plans to meet the public's clamor for action and to mobilize support. Yet the premature airing of proposed measures may alert adversaries and jeopardize a plan's success.

The most dramatic example of this dilemma for Nixon occurred not when he was president, but when he was a presidential candidate in October 1960. In a world divided by the Cold War, the inexperienced Kennedy was a question mark compared with the Vice President, whose travels abroad had brought him international prestige. The Communist-organized

riots against the Vice President in Caracas in 1958, and then his
Kitchen Debate with Khrushchev in 1959, had served to
enhance Nixon's credentials as a future leader of the Free
World.

Furthermore, Kennedy had sullied his reputation on foreign policy with two statements. After the U-2 spy plane was
brought down in Russia in May 1960, Senator Kennedy suggested that President Eisenhower should "express regrets to
Chairman Khrushchev." Kennedy was stung by the charge
that he had asked Eisenhower to apologize to the Communists. The unarmed plane had been relaying needed intelligence of Soviet missile and deployment sites.

Secondly, in his third debate with Nixon, Kennedy suggested that Formosa's offshore islands, Quemoy and Matsu,
were not worth defending. Again, Kennedy managed to look
irresolute and weak in foreign policy compared with Vice
President Nixon.

Despite Kennedy's "victory" in the famous first televised
debate in September, polls a month later revealed that his
stand on Quemoy and Matsu was causing him slippage in
public opinion. Nixon had said, "My administration will not
give an island or inch to Communists." The momentum now
was with Nixon, who was rapidly closing the gap.

At the American Legion Convention in Miami on October
18, Nixon would hit again on Kennedy's vulnerability in foreign affairs. The topic was Cuba. In Kennedy's book of
speeches published the previous winter, the Senator had
described Fidel Castro as a worthy "heir of Simón Bolívar."
Kennedy had been reflecting the tenor of the *New York Times*
Latin American affairs writer David Matthews, who had
hailed Castro as "a freedom-loving democrat."

"Castro was not," said Nixon in Miami, "a rebel in the tradition of Bolívar."

When Vice President Nixon met Premier Fidel Castro during his first visit to the United States in April 1957, Nixon had written that Castro "was either incredibly naive about Communism or under Communist discipline." Such a view was, at that time, opposed by the Latin American bureau of the State Department. The official State Department line was to "try to get along with Castro and understand him," despite two former U.S. ambassadors to Cuba who agreed with Nixon's reasoning.

By early 1960, the Eisenhower administration had adopted Nixon's view. In February, the CIA was given instructions to provide arms, ammunition, and training for Cubans who had fled the Castro regime and were in exile in the United States.

At the time of the debates, the program had been in place for six months, but Nixon was not allowed to make mention of this covert operation.

Privately, Nixon argued to the National Security Council that the administration could adopt a greater public posture against Castro without revealing the secret plans for invasion. When Nixon received approval for outlining such measures, he chose the American Legion Convention in Miami as his forum. The audience of veterans in this city closest to Cuba greeted enthusiastically Nixon's policy for a "quarantine for Cuba." Nixon recommended economic, political, and diplomatic isolation of Cuba. He added that "the time for patience was past," and that we should move vigorously in full association of our sister Latin American republics "to eradicate this cancer" in our hemisphere and "to prevent further Soviet penetration." "The Administration," said Nixon, was planning "a number of steps" and "will very promptly take the strongest possible economic measures to counter the economic banditry being practiced by this regime against our citizens."

Two days later, just before the fourth debate, Kennedy was able to trump Nixon's "quarantine speech." On October 20, the headlines of the *Scripps-Howard* papers, to whom the Senator had given an exclusive story, blared: "Kennedy Advocates U.S. Intervention in Cuba; Calls for Aid to Rebel Forces in Cuba."

In the interview, Kennedy went on to say, "We must attempt to strengthen the non-Batista democratic anti-Castro forces in exile and in Cuba itself, who offer eventual hope for overthrowing Castro. Thus far, these fighters for freedom have had no support from our government."

Nixon smelled a rat. He asked a top aide to call the White House to find out if Kennedy—in the customary top security briefing that is available for any presidential nominee—had been informed by CIA Director Allen Dulles of the training being given to refugees during the last few months in preparation of invasion of Cuba.

The answer was yes. Nixon, in *Six Crises*, writes, "For the first and only time in the campaign, I got mad at Kennedy personally." Kennedy was exploiting the private briefing to earn political points. Kennedy's call for intervention was jeopardizing the security of a United States foreign policy operation. Nixon added, "My rage was greater because I could do nothing about it."

Nixon was faced with a dilemma. Kennedy had read the same polls as Nixon, which reported that American voters favored a tougher line against Castro. Within the councils of state, Nixon had long pushed for such an aggressive policy, and partially because of his efforts, the secret training of exiles was now in progress. Of course, Nixon could have just stated that Kennedy was only advocating a policy that already was in preparation at his own urging. But, Nixon wrote later, "That would have been utterly irresponsible: it would have disclosed a secret operation and would have completely destroyed its effectiveness."

To protect the security of the proposed invasion, Nixon took the other extreme. He attacked the Kennedy position as wrong and irresponsible because it would violate our treaty agreements. At the fourth debate, on October 21, in New York, when Kennedy reasserted his proposal for intervention, Nixon answered: "I think that Senator Kennedy's policies and recommendations for the handling of the Castro regime are probably the most dangerously irresponsible recommendations that he's made during the course of this campaign."

Nixon was dead right in that accusation, but he could not give the real reason why Kennedy was so "irresponsible."

Instead, he took this tack:

> If we were to follow that recommendation . . . we would lose all our friends in Latin America, we would probably be condemned in the United Nations, and we would not accomplish our objective. . . . It would be an open invitation for Mr. Khrushchev . . . to come into Latin America and to engage in what would be a civil war and possibly even worse than that.

Nixon's words were effective—they silenced Kennedy. Ironically, Nixon was praised for his statesmanship by his usual liberal media foes. James Reston of *The New York Times* said, "The Vice-President's criticism of Senator Kennedy's program for assisting anti-Castro forces to regain power was approved by well-informed people tonight." The *Washington Post* noted, "Mr. Nixon accused Mr. Kennedy of recklessness, and there is a good deal of point to this observation. . . . Mr. Nixon made a sound point about avoiding unilateral intervention."

Two days later, the Senator backtracked. In a brief statement to the press, he said, "I have never advocated, and I do not now advocate, intervention in Cuba in violation of our treaty obligations."

Nixon may have won some editorial praise from sources

not usually friendly to his aspirations. Yet in the public perception, Kennedy was the winner. Sixty million people heard him on television strike a tougher pose against communism than Nixon. The few liberal newspapers that praised Nixon's position ended up opposing his candidacy editorially.

Nixon knew that any public acknowledgment of the CIA operation would "destroy its ability to get the job done" in Cuba. To have mentioned, even indirectly, contingent military plans and his role in shaping them, would have checkmated Kennedy, but at the risk of alerting Cuba. In choosing to maintain its secrecy, Nixon revealed his statesmanship, even when it may have contributed to his hairline defeat by Kennedy.

Neville Chamberlain

Winston Churchill once jibed, "An empty cab pulled up to 10 Downing Street and Neville Chamberlain stepped out." It was a cruel comment revealing Churchill's belief that Chamberlain was devoid of any real knowledge about foreign policy. Yet if "empty" meant lacking in solid convictions, Churchill was unfair to the new British prime minister, who succeeded Stanley Baldwin in February 1937.

Chamberlain was every bit as resolute in his beliefs as Churchill and was viewed by his countrymen as far more reliable. If colorless, Chamberlain was considered a man of sturdy dependability, while the flamboyant Churchill was often viewed as a loose cannon on the deck.

As the former chancellor of the exchequer, Chamberlain had built his reputation as a solid man on economic issues. He had started his political life as a mayor of Birmingham. Though he had little experience in foreign affairs, Chamberlain told his foreign secretary, Anthony Eden, whom he had inherited from the Baldwin government, "I know you won't mind if I take a lot more interest in foreign affairs . . . like S.B. [Stanley Baldwin]" In other words, as Chamberlain told his family, he was going to be his own foreign secretary. When Chamberlain moved into 10 Downing Street, he saw little likelihood of war: first, because Britain's military alliance with France was a deterrent to war by Germany; second, because he thought Herr Hitler was not an unreasonable man and that he personally could come to some kind of accommodation with him; and third and most important, because he thought that a second world war in Europe was too dreadful a prospect for anyone to risk.

On Friday, March 11, 1938, Chamberlain gave a luncheon for German foreign secretary Ribbentrop. He said to tell Herr Hitler "that it had always been my desire to clear up German-British relations." At that very time, German troops were secretly assembling on the Austrian borders. Two days later, the German army marched into Vienna.

Chamberlain had not believed Foreign Secretary Eden two months earlier when he had warned that Hitler had made a deal with Mussolini for the German *Anschluss* of Austria. So Eden had resigned in protest.

The forced annexation of Austria by Germany shook Chamberlain but did not shatter his faith that Hitler could be deterred from starting a war. Yet the German seizure of Austria now made the situation of its neighbor, Czechoslovakia, more precarious. Over three million of its citizens—about 23 percent of the total population—were German speakers who lived in the western regions of Czechoslovakia called the Sudetenland. Hitler was making speeches demanding the incorporation of the Sudetenland in the greater Reich of Germany and Austria and threatening military action to achieve his goal.

The problem for Chamberlain was that France had signed

a pact to defend Czechoslovakia against any German invasion, and Britain was bound by treaty to join France in case of
war against Germany.

For too long, Britain had closed its eyes to the reappearance
of a military Germany under Hitler, and its state of armament
reflected its dilatory response.

After the Hitler annexation of Austria, Churchill from the
back bench said:

> I have watched this famous island descending fecklessly
> the stairway which leads to a dark gulf. It is a fine brass
> stairway at the beginning, but after a bit the carpet
> ends. And a little farther on still, these break beneath
> your feet. . . .
>
> Look back upon the last five years—since, that is to
> say, when Germany began to rearm in earnest and
> openly seek revenge.

Churchill's jeremiad against the lassitude of the British
government did not find resonance in his country. True,
Churchill, the lonely prophet in the wilderness for most of the
thirties, had been winning a few Conservative members to his
view that Hitler was a madman and that war was a probability
unless a rearmed Britain stood up to the Nazi führer. But
Chamberlain began to worry about the slippage in his support. His former foreign secretary, the dashing young Anthony
Eden, had just joined the swell of dissent.

Though no orator, Chamberlain believed he could seize
the initiative from the Churchill group. He was, after all, the
prime minister. He was still more popular than the volatile
Churchill, and he had the issue: peace.

On September 12, Hitler ranted to his frenzied followers at
a massive Nazi rally that the Sudetenland Germans in
Czechoslovakia must be given "self-determination" immedi-

ately. If Hitler enforced that demand by marching in troops, and France responded by coming to the aid of the besieged Czech nation, world war was imminent.

Chamberlain told his foreign minister and cabinet that he would go to Germany and personally convince Hitler to pull back from the brink of war. Though his foreign office had dropped hints of Chamberlain's eagerness to see the German leader, no interest was shown by Hitler. Chamberlain told his foreign secretary, Lord Halifax, that he would fly unannounced to Germany even without an invitation. A dumbfounded Halifax dissuaded him, suggesting that a British prime minister cannot leave the country without the consent of the sovereign. Chamberlain relented but wrote to King George VI that he was considering a trip to Germany.

Finally, an invitation came from Hitler to visit him at his mountain retreat, Berchtesgaden. Their meeting convinced Chamberlain that Hitler's ambitions were confined to the Sudetenland. Chamberlain told his cabinet colleagues that "Hitler was a nervous, excitable man, but that he doesn't want war and only wants the Sudetenland dispute settled."

Chamberlain again went to visit Hitler—this time at the spa Bad Godesberg—to receive more assurances. On this occasion, Hitler reneged on his earlier statement. The time, said Hitler, for making concessions on the Sudetenland had passed.

Chamberlain returned on September 24 to London to begin a round of gloomy deliberations with the cabinet, while on the same day in Berlin, Adolf Hitler roared his denunciation of the Czechs and defiance of the world. The next day, Chamberlain sat before a BBC radio microphone and spoke wearily and desperately of war incredibly looming because of "a quarrel in a far-away country between people of whom we know nothing."

On September 26, President Franklin Roosevelt sent a

public telegram to Chamberlain, Hitler, Premier Daladier of France, and others, appealing that the parties "not break off negotiations, looking to a peaceful, fair, and constructive settlement of the questions at issue."

Chamberlain had his answer. He would propose a peace conference of the principal parties. He instructed his ambassador in Rome to ask Mussolini to ask Hitler to agree.

His ambassador to Germany, Neville Henderson, carried this formal proposal from Chamberlain: "I am ready to come to Berlin myself at once to discuss arrangements for the transfer [of the Sudetenland] with you and representatives of the Czech Government, together with representatives of France and Italy, if you desire."

As clouds of war darkened over London, the House of Commons met. Every seat in the visitors' gallery, including those of the Queen Mother and the Archbishop of Canterbury, was taken. A hush settled over the chamber as the Prime Minister rose. "I have now been informed by Herr Hitler that he invites me to meet him at Munich tomorrow morning. He has also invited Signor Mussolini and Monsieur Daladier. . . . I need not say what my answer will be."

Then a cry issued forth from the chamber by a member: "Thank God for the Prime Minister!"

Chamberlain continued: "We are all patriots, and there can be no Honourable Member of this House who did not feel his heart leap that this crisis has been postponed to give us once more an opportunity to try what reason and good will and discussion will do to settle a problem which now is in sight of settlement."

Chamberlain then told the House what it wanted to hear: he was going to Berlin and would return with peace.

The response was tumultuous. The House rose in a formal demonstration of relief, approval, and praise. Only the Churchill supporters, former foreign secretary Anthony Eden, and author Harold Nicolson, uttered warnings.

Chamberlain returned to 10 Downing Street to find a congratulatory telegram from President Roosevelt. Crowds gathered around the residence. From his study, Chamberlain could hear the cries, "God bless Neville," "Good old Neville," "Neville, you did it."

Although Chamberlain hated to fly, the seventy-year-old was jaunty as he gave the cheering crowd at Heston Airport this allusion to Shakespeare: "When I come back, I hope I might be able to say, as Hotspur says in *Henry IV,* 'Out of this nettle, danger, we pluck the flower safety.' "

His listeners roared. Their cries reflected the hopes of a nation that Chamberlain's mission to Munich would avert war. Chamberlain had put the word "peace" on the lips of all Britons before he even left for Germany. His public declaration made any private negotiation with the Nazi dictator a mockery. It would not be a discussion of issues but a dictation of terms by Hitler.

The 1938 meeting of Chamberlain and Daladier with Hitler and Mussolini is called the Munich Conference, but it was more a dance than a "conference," with Hitler orchestrating the music, writing the words, and choreographing the steps.

First of all, it was held not in the capital of Germany, Berlin, at the chancery, but in Munich, at the Brown House, the birthplace of the Nazi Party; specifically, in Hitler's old office, now named the *Führerbau.*

Chamberlain was the first to arrive. Next was Premier Daladier of France. They were greeted not by Hitler himself, but by a host of black-uniformed SS men, every one the image of stiff, heel-clicking pomposity.

Then Hermann Göring arrived, resplendent in a white

uniform that did nothing to diminish his girth. The visiting dignitaries picked at the buffet of knockwurst, bratwurst, red cabbage, and other Bavarian delights, while awaiting the Führer. Then Mussolini entered as if paving the way for his fellow fascist dictator.

When Hitler arrived, he did not join the rest at the refectory table, but led them into his office. There was no long green table equipped with name cards, tablets, or freshly sharpened pencils—only a small round table in front of his desk. Without amenities, Hitler opened the meeting with a diatribe against Czechoslovakia, spreading his arms and clenching his fists. He ended with the injunction that the German occupation of the Sudetenland must begin at once.

Then Mussolini followed his script by pulling a draft for terms of settlement that had been prepared earlier with Hitler's approval. Chamberlain looked at it and expressed unwillingness to agree unless the Czech government accepted it, so he urged that a Czech representative attend the conference. Hitler's response was another tirade against the Czechs. He ended saying that no Czech representative was "available" and that there would be no "consulting with the Czechs on every detail." The meeting adjourned on that note.

If the Czechs were not to be consulted, Chamberlain himself had to convince them to accept the settlement. He telegraphed them a guarantee that Hitler would not move his troops beyond the Sudetenland. A dispirited Czech government reluctantly acceded, knowing that their ally France had abandoned them.

In the morning, Chamberlain went to Hitler's private apartment. A sullen Hitler let Chamberlain do the talking. When Chamberlain asked for assurances that Germany would never try to occupy all of Czechoslovakia, Hitler muttered "Ja, ja," and said, "Let me sign the document."

Chamberlain, on the return trip to London, felt tired but

triumphant. On his arrival at Heston Airport, there was a command invitation from King George VI "to come straight to Buckingham Palace so that I can express to you personally my most heartfelt congratulations on the success of your visit to Munich."

On the way to the palace, the streets were lined with crowds shouting themselves hoarse—leaping on the running boards of the limousine and thrusting their hands through the window to shake hands with the Prime Minister.

At the palace, Chamberlain appeared on the royal balcony with the King and Queen. Afterward, he returned to 10 Downing Street for a meeting with his cabinet. The ministers were waiting outside the door to greet him.

Waving the piece of paper that he and Adolf Hitler had signed that morning, he cited the words Prime Minister Benjamin Disraeli had used in 1878 when he returned from Germany with a treaty that concluded the Russo-Turkish War: "My good friends, for the second time in our history, a British Prime Minister has returned from Germany bringing 'peace with honour.' I believe it is peace for our time."

On October 2, the settlement carried the House of Commons overwhelmingly. Churchill, however, from the back benches said, "It is a disaster of the first magnitude," adding, "it is the first foretaste of a bitter cup which will be proffered to us year by year unless by a supreme recovery of our usual health and martial vigor, we rise again and take our stand for freedom as in the olden times."

In the sweet jubilation that greeted the Prime Minister's peace settlement, the admonitions of Churchill and his cadre were considered a sour note. Lady Margaret Oxford, a member of the House of Commons, said, "Chamberlain is the greatest Englishman who ever lived." When Lady Astor, a frequent Churchill foe, lauded Chamberlain as a "Prince of Peace," Churchill muttered, "I thought the Prince of Peace came from Bethlehem, not Birmingham [Chamberlain's birth-place]."

In a more serious tone, he told his followers, "Neville had the choice between war and dishonour. He chose dishonour and he will get war anyway."

Chamberlain, of course, thought he had chosen peace, and he had spotlighted that as his objective before he left for the conference table. Any concessions he might possibly have extracted from Hitler, he conceded in advance. He came to Munich to purchase peace, for which he would pay any price.

Churchill described the puritanical Chamberlain in the days leading to Munich: "He has a lust for peace." By parading that craving, Chamberlain let Hitler dictate the terms of capitulation.

Chester Karrass, a world expert on business negotiation, devotes a chapter in his book *Negotiating Game* to Chamberlain and the Munich settlement. As he points out, Chamberlain frittered away a strong bargaining position in his frenzy to avert war.

The Czechs—a million strong—were ready to fight from mountain fortresses. The French were prepared to add one hundred divisions to the field. Together, they outnumbered the Nazis two to one. British Intelligence had revealed to Chamberlain that many anti-Nazi generals had proposed to destroy Hitler if the Allies would commit themselves to resist the Czech takeover.

Yet Chamberlain put himself in the role of a supplicant—traveling to Germany and negotiating on Hitler's ground in Hitler's home office with Mussolini as a mediator. Karrass says, "In negotiation, as in life, nice guys do win their objectives when they know what they are doing." Chamberlain thought he knew what he was doing—securing peace—but he let the whole world, including Hitler, know that he would pay any price for peace. He let the glare of advance publicity smother the prospect for peace.

It is one thing for a lawyer in a divorce settlement proceeding to make inflated demands over the telephone to the opposing lawyer, but it is quite another thing for the union head to scream into a microphone before hundreds of its members impossible terms that impede constructive bargaining, with the result of denying members any betterment of conditions, or worse, removal of the company to a more hospitable clime. Churchill said, "Perfection is the enemy of progress," and promises made to the press of unrealistic results are bad politics as well as bad business. Publicity is a heady tonic for leaders and chief executives. But when headlines mean a powerless position at the bargaining table, they can be a bankrupting luxury. Advance publicity may jeopardize the success of a company's marketing of a new product's development or a new project's plans. As in the case of Kennedy and the secret Cuba operation, such publicity is worse than counterproductive. It is shortsighted and stupid.

V

NEVER GIVE UP UNILATERALLY WHAT COULD BE USED AS A BARGAINING CHIP. MAKE YOUR ADVERSARIES GIVE SOMETHING FOR EVERYTHING THEY GET.

Nixon

It is more blessed to give than to receive," Jesus urged in the Sermons on the Mount. Yet in his almanac of business advice, Benjamin Franklin had Poor Richard admonish, "Only give in on smaller points in order to gain in larger ones."

When Nixon was practicing law with Nixon, Mudge, Rose, Guthrie and Alexander in New York in the 1960s, he gave me this practical counsel concerning some negotiations in which I was involved:

1. Get something for every concession. Don't think you have to give tit for tat. Don't feel you have to split fifty-fifty. If he gives sixty, give him forty.
2. Make concessions that give nothing away.
3. Conserve your concessions.

Nixon hoped his administration would be remembered as one that "turned the era of confrontation into the era of negotiation." In other words, he wanted to defuse the Cold War into some kind of détente. His strategy of "triangularization" was aimed at reshaping a bipolar world into a three-sided one, led by the Soviet Union, the United States, and mainland China. Before this could happen, Nixon needed to establish a diplomatic office in Beijing, replacing the indirect and mostly ineffectual back channels and third-party arbitration between the two countries.

Of course, he could have followed the example of the British and French, who recognized Red China and abandoned the Nationalist Chinese government in Taiwan. But such a move would mean canceling our defense treaties with Taiwan and implicitly endorsing Red China's claim to the island formerly known as Formosa. In addition, the State Department suspected that even the desertion of Taiwan would not be enough for the People's Republic to accept an exchange of ambassadors. The United States would also have to cease its support of South Vietnam and pull out of Southeast Asia.

The genius of Nixon's negotiations enabled him to have his cake and eat it too. That is, he achieved "triangularization" without abandonment of U.S. military support of Taiwan. In Chou En-lai, Nixon found a most fascinating political personality. Churchill and de Gaulle awed him, but they were a generation older with their heroic accomplishments in World War II. Chou En-lai was Nixon's contemporary, with all the sophistication of a cultured world traveler that clothed a savagery of the most ruthless general. He did not radiate the bigger-than-life presence of Mao, whose health prevented him from handling the day-to-day negotiating of details. Mao was blunt, whereas Chou was subtle, with a mind as sinuous as a labyrinth.

In their meetings with Chairman Mao Tse-tung and Premier Chou En-lai, Nixon and Kissinger affirmed the United

States' belief in "one China," a concept championed by both the Red Chinese and the Nationalist Chinese and in the principle that the settlement of those differences between the two competing governments could be achieved only by "peaceful resolution."

"Peaceful" was the operative word. It allowed the United States to continue its defense treaties with Taiwan. If Red China were to launch a military attack to reclaim Taiwan, the United States would side with the Nationalist government to defend against such aggression.

With those carefully crafted phrases, "one China" and "peaceful resolution," Nixon gained a liaison office in Beijing. George Bush would be the first liaison officer of that mission in Beijing. This access to the People's Republic was a success that exceeded Nixon's greatest hopes. The United States, through the liaison office, developed a warmer working relationship with the People's Republic than either Britain or France had built with their embassies (not to mention the Soviet Union).

The United States became the pivotal middleman of the "triangle," far closer to both than the Marxist regimes were to each other—despite both nations' support of North Vietnam.

In principle, Nixon was not opposed to the advancement of the liaison office into an embassy in due time. However, since the United States was already enjoying a better ongoing relationship with the People's Republic than any other western democracy, Nixon did not see the immediate advantage in elevating the liaison office to an embassy. The People's Republic, while satisfied with how well the liaison mission was working in developing an ongoing relationship, wanted the upgrade to an embassy, both for its symbolic importance and its rejection of the Nationalist China of Taiwan.

Nixon let the question of full diplomatic status dangle unanswered. The establishment of an embassy would have been seen by China as a friendly gesture but by Russia as a hostile signal. The issue afforded Nixon more leverage if left unresolved. In the future, if he did decide to grant embassy status, it would be coupled with a quid pro quo negotiation with the People's Republic. Nixon was not going to make a gift of a bargaining chip. Secretary of State Henry Kissinger would continue this policy under President Ford.

The power-brokering diplomacy of Nixon and Kissinger finally came to a head under the Carter administration. From the very beginning, both President Carter and his secretary of state, Cyrus Vance, were leaning toward giving full recognition to China. But National Security Chief Zbigniew Brzezinski, the émigré from Communist Poland, strongly opposed such a move.

In his first major foreign policy address as president on May 17, 1977, Carter declared that anti-Communism had ceased to be a dominant factor in foreign policy. America, said Carter, had too long suffered from "an inordinate fear of Communism." In Vienna, President Carter literally hugged and kissed Chairman Brezhnev. The Kremlin, however, perceived an irresolute president who would not resist a Soviet expansion of influence.

Aggressive moves by the Soviet Union in 1978 changed Zbigniew Brzezinski's mind about China. The Russians were fighting in Afghanistan to preserve their puppet regime. They had intervened in Africa, toppling the pro-Western kingdoms of Yemen and Ethiopia and had replaced them with Communist military dictatorships answerable to the Kremlin. And they were militarily equipping Cuban troops dispatched by Castro to overthrow the Angolan government, which had been friendly with the West. Furthermore, Chairman Leonid Brezhnev slammed the door on discussions of nuclear arms limitation.

President Carter now saw the United States being perceived as "a helpless, pitiful giant"—an allusion to Swift's Gulliver—bullied by the Soviet Union. He readily adopted Brzezinski's revised recommendation about a change in our diplomatic status in Beijing. Brzezinski, like Kissinger before him, traveled to the People's Republic in 1979 to discuss the matter. In Beijing, Brzezinski made his historic riposte to Russia, "America has made up its mind."

President Carter played the announcement of the diplomatic recognition of China for all it was worth. With drama, the White House had asked the three television networks for a time slot during which the President would speak on an undisclosed subject. After an eight-minute speech, Carter leaned back in his chair, unaware that the microphone was still on. With a touch of smugness, the President said, almost to himself, "Massive applause throughout the nation." But the applause was far from universal. John B. Oakes, former senior editor of *The New York Times*, wrote that "by taking the action in the way he had taken it, President Carter had seriously undermined pretensions to be the moral leader of the world and an exemplar of constancy and faithfulness to our friends."

In a way, Carter and Brzezinski thought they were replicating Nixon and Kissinger's strategy seven years earlier. Increasing our access to China would make Russia a more responsible and more flexible adversary in a disintegrating détente.

But, whereas Nixon's reaching out to China had all the finesse of a rapier, Brzezinski caused the slam of a sledgehammer. Instead of making Russia more amenable, the move made the Soviet Union all the more aggressive. The Soviets did not back away from their subversive and military operations in Africa, but instead built up the pressure. They raised the decibel volume of their anti-West propaganda drive. If elevating the Liaison Office to embassy status was designed to trigger a more conciliatory Russian foreign policy, it backfired. Carter had thought that playing "the China card" would induce Moscow into the signing of SALT II. Brezhnev said, "Nyet."

In his memoirs, President Carter lists the according of embassy recognition to the People's Republic as one of his foreign policy achievements. Yet no negotiating skills were required in making a one-sided concession. It was a gift rather than a trade-off.

It was a costly gift at that. Embassy status for the People's Republic of China required the renunciation of our diplomatic ties with Nationalist China in Taiwan. Its ambassador was told of the decision only one hour before Carter went on television—a gratuitous insult to old allies. Later, Congress, without presidential initiative, passed some measures in an attempt to redress the military vulnerability of Taiwan. Nevertheless, the embassy move debased the status of a loyal ally and did not appreciably strengthen our already successful working relationship with the mainland Chinese.

The Carter administration rationalized their diplomatic move as an opening up of trade and investment opportunities in the world's largest nation. Yet to this day, our trade imbalance with China is worse than that with Japan.

Nixon's opening relations with the People's Republic was based not on economics but on geopolitics. He once said to Kissinger after his Beijing Agreement of 1972 was announced, "Henry, you know I have hundreds of garment manufacturers pressing me about Chinese factories. I didn't open up China to please the pajama makers. It was a power move."

In truth, Brzezinski's decision to give embassy status was also geopolitical. It was a shot across the bow of the Soviet Union. But because the United States already had a working arrangement with the People's Republic, it was a hollow gesture that the Soviets interpreted as hostile, and they reacted accordingly.

Critics have charged that Carter, like Esau, sold out Taiwan "for a mess of pottage." Carter had frittered away a bargaining chip and received something negligible in return. As former Chinese liaison George Bush said, "We gave all and got nothing." China, mired in a backward rural economy, could offer few real business investment opportunities. To allow some capitalism and American investment in their country was not a concession on their part, but a gift on our part.

Benjamin Franklin

If Ronald Reagan was the Great Communicator, Benjamin Franklin was the Great Negotiator. He was the only principal player in and signer of all five documents that created America: the Declaration of Independence; the Articles of Confederation; the treaty with France that recognized the United States as a sovereign nation; the treaty to conclude the war with England; and the Constitution.

Before America even declared its independence, Franklin was, in a sense, its first diplomat. Franklin had been retained by three colonies to argue their cases in London to Parliament and the King's ministers. Today we would call his role in attempting to change the tax policy of the British government that of a lobbyist. Franklin would confess failure in that mission.

The culmination of his abortive endeavor was the Cockpit Affair. In a star-chamber proceeding, the King's attorney general, Alexander Wedderburn, announced trumped-up charges against a lawyerless Franklin, seated in the defendant's dock. The King's plan was to incite Franklin into a response that would justify a jail sentence for contempt. In a three-hour diatribe, Wedderburn depicted Franklin as not only the instigator of every colonial protest and every British shipment thrown into the sea, but also as a taker of bribes and perpetrator of bastardy. In the end, when Wedderburn could trigger no rise, he concluded with the trilled r's of his Scottish burr, "Franklin, you are less than a traitor—you are nothing but a common fornicator and thief." Franklin maintained a bemused and weary smile. But afterward, Franklin caught Wedderburn in the lobby and said, "Anyone who strikes a man who can't strike back is less than a man. But when we Americans do strike back, you will find yourself a lesser man serving a King with a lesser empire."

Patience was only one of Franklin's paramount skills as a diplomat. He was also a superb bargainer, crafter of compromise, and drafter of precise or ambiguous language, as the case called for. (In editing Jefferson's Declaration of Independence, he came up with the phrase "pursuit of happiness.") All of these negotiating arts were needed for the treaty of Paris that formally ended the War of Independence and secured the recognition by Britain of the new American nation.

Lord Cornwallis had surrendered to General Washington at Yorktown, but that did not mean that Britain had to surrender the claims of damages by those American colonists who had remained loyal to the crown. Neither did Britain have to give up its territory west of the colonies stretching to the Mississippi. The nation that "ruled the waves" did not have to yield whaling and fishing rights off the coasts of Nova Scotia nor even have to recognize America's rights to the seas for trade and commerce.

Despite the American victory, Britain still was the most formidable military power in the world. The fledgling United States was bankrupt. Its armies had disbanded, and it had no navy. Despite diplomatic pressure from France, Spain, and the Netherlands, Britain had no compelling interest forcing it to sign a treaty that recognized the United States. Britain could choose to leave the Americans in limbo.

The greatest asset the U.S. commissioners brought to the negotiating table in Paris was Benjamin Franklin himself. He was the only one of the commissioners to remain in France for the entire duration of the discussions and the only one with clear goals: recognition by Great Britain, American title to the western territories, and no reparations for American Tories.

The lawyer John Jay was obsessed by the slight that Britain had given him and the other commissioners by receiving them as agents of the colonies instead of as representatives of the United States. John Adams concentrated his energies on securing fishing rights for his fellow New Englanders, and Thomas Jefferson never showed up.

Franklin was a presence in Paris. From the very day he arrived in Versailles in 1776 to press the colonial case before King Louis XVI, he charmed the Parisians. A master of public relations, Franklin knew how to make a splash by understatement. Before a court that bedecked themselves with perfumed perukes, silken shirts, and velvet tights, Franklin came wigless in plain spun muslin. In the court that foreshadowed the recent fad of radical chic, Franklin seemed to embody the Rousseau ideal of the natural man, and he exploited that image.

His accomplishments as a scientist—his experiments in electricity, his discovery of the Gulf Stream, and his sighting of a continental drift—had been noted. Also known were his skills as an inventor—he had introduced bifocals, designed the Franklin stove, and fashioned the armonica, a musical instrument for which Mozart and Beethoven composed. Finally, the French translation of his Poor Richard's sayings was immensely popular. In short, Franklin was America's first pop idol export.

Ostensibly, the talks in Paris were bilateral—between Britain and America—but actually they were trilateral, because the Treaty of Alliance with France that Franklin negotiated in 1777 forbade either party to conclude a separate peace with Britain. By those terms, the American commissioners were to make no moves contrary to the advice of the French king.

In one demand, Franklin was curiously unmovable. Neither Jay nor Adams was as adamant as Franklin on the subject of the damages claimed by the American Tories. Perhaps Franklin's sensitivity on the subject can be explained by the fact that his only son, William, was one of the Tories.

When Franklin returned to Philadelphia from London in 1777 after lobbying in vain against the crown's taxes, he was greeted by his daughter, who tearfully informed him that his wife had died and his son had become a Tory.

The British crown played on Franklin's insecurities by appointing William the royal governor of New Jersey. His name, they knew, was a powerful propaganda weapon in the cause of the crown. William Franklin, in turn, relished being invested with the robes and seals of office.

His father traveled directly to Trenton upon hearing the news. "Billy," he reportedly said, "if you choose the King as your master, you will lose me as your father."

They never saw each other again, although after the war, Billy attempted a reconciliation. His father's response was cordial but cold—perhaps because along with the pleas to his father was an entreaty to him as commissioner not to deal harshly with Americans who sided, as he had, with King George III.

But Franklin deemed the support of the King by his close friends, as well as his son, as the worst sort of betrayal. He once wrote on the subject of reparations, "We are commanded to forgive our enemies, but we are nowhere commanded to forgive our friends."

Article X of the capitulation signed at Yorktown decreed that all loyalists would be dealt with according to the laws of their respective states. Since the British command in New York had made no provision to evacuate the loyalists to safety, widespread panic ensued as soon as the magnitude of the defeat became known. William Franklin, if taken in New Jersey, could expect to be hanged for treason. He had escaped to London, however.

As the new British prime minister, Lord Shelburne had succeeded Lord Rockingham in 1782. Benjamin Franklin knew Shelburne and respected him because he didn't bear the animosity toward the colonists his predecessor had. The replacement of the recalcitrant Rockingham would ease the course of negotiations.

Shelburne did, however, reflect the adamant concern of the court that those who maintained their allegiance to the crown should not suffer for their loyalty. In fact, Franklin and the other commissioners had no appetite for harsh revenge. But Franklin, in particular, bridled at the thought of reparations for damages. The very suggestion that the penniless new republic should issue promissory claims to American Tories for damages to their properties or businesses enraged him. What about the losses Americans sustained when their houses were occupied or destroyed, their goods confiscated, or their crops stolen? Franklin had been methodically compiling notes of these damages and losses. As the former postmaster general, Franklin had an extensive network of friends in all the thirteen colonies who forwarded their financial grievances to him.*

Franklin was fully prepared to present Henry Oswald, Prime Minister Shelburne's envoy, with these itemized bills. Adams dissuaded him in the fear that such a bald demand

---

* Perhaps because of his travels through all the colonies in his organization of a mailing system, Franklin was the first to call himself an American when Washington introduced himself as a Virginian and John Adams called himself a Massachusetts man.

would so antagonize the British that they would refuse even to come to Paris to negotiate. Franklin acquiesced.

In preparation for bargaining, Franklin drafted a memorandum that outlined four points on which there would be no compromise. First, the withdrawal of all British troops (in various regions of the colonies, such as New York and enclaves in the south that were pockets of Tory sympathy, some troops remained to protect loyalists from acts of retribution); second, the settlement of the boundaries of the thirteen colonies; third, the assigning to the new American states the Mississippi territory that the French had ceded to the British in the Treaty of 1763 concluding the Seven Years' War (with the exception of French-speaking Canada); and fourth, fishing and whaling rights on the Newfoundland banks.

The English envoy took back these demands to Shelburne just as the news arrived that the British had beaten back a Franco-Spanish naval assault in Gibraltar. The strengthened British hand seemed to endanger the acceptance of the American demands.

Franklin, who was always considered too pro-French by Jay and Adams, now met secretly with the British. By excluding their historic enemy, Franklin ingratiated himself with the British, who saw an opportunity to split the Franco-American alliance.

By playing off the English against the French, Franklin extracted a reluctant consent from Shelburne. His assent to Franklin's stiff demands created the perception that he had been badly outbargained and almost toppled his prime ministership.

Meanwhile, Prime Minister Vergennes was outraged upon learning of Franklin's dealing behind his back. In reply, Franklin crafted a superb diplomatic argument to the French: if they protested, they would only be signaling to the British that they had succeeded in overturning the Franco-American alliance. As he told Vergennes, "The English, I just now learn, flatter themselves that they have already divided us."

Although the English had agreed to the treaty based on the four Franklin points, they now felt themselves duped by the wily Franklin. The foreign secretary, Thomas Grenville, now balked at signing the treaty in Paris, proclaiming that the British signature was contingent on American agreement to give reparations to the loyalists.

It was at this crucial point that Benjamin Franklin pulled from his briefcase the itemized bills of every colonist's house burned, warehouses confiscated, horses requisitioned, ship goods seized, and crops destroyed and seized by the British.

Franklin had not given away that bargaining chip, and his timely presentation of the bill caused the British to relent.

In September 1783, they signed. Franklin wore his old green Manchester suit at the ceremony. Adams thought the shabby coat inappropriate for such an event. Franklin explained that he had worn that same suit eight years earlier, in the twelve-hour grilling he had undergone in the star-chamber proceeding of the Cockpit Affair. Franklin then told Adams, "I just had to give my old suit a little revenge."

Franklin was a scientist, inventor, author, philosopher, and statesman, but he was also a businessman, and a canny one. Of the Founding Fathers, he was the only poor boy who rose to become the equivalent of a millionaire and retire at the age of forty-five. Franklin was the first American who figured out the concept of vertical monopoly. When the price of paper began squeezing him, he bought his own forest and operated his own sawmills. Franklin was also the first in the world to franchise himself. He had Franklin printing and stationery shops in New York, Charleston, Bermuda, and elsewhere. He also devised the first mail order catalog.

It figures then that Franklin was a shrewd bargainer. He

never gave away a penny in a deal, and he made the other side sweat for everything it got.

Though he flashed a warm smile, he had a cold eye for the dollar. When he possessed something the other side wanted or something they feared, he did not give it away, rather he preserved and polished his advantage. He knew that when you give advantages away, you don't win popularity but lose respect. As a merchant in Philadelphia drawing up sales contracts and as a mediator in Paris drafting treaty terms, Franklin held the strength of his cards close to his chest.

VI

NEVER LET YOUR ADVERSARY UNDERESTIMATE WHAT YOU WOULD DO IN RESPONSE TO A CHALLENGE. NEVER TELL HIM WHAT YOU WOULD NOT DO.

Nixon

In his Iron Curtain address at Fulton, Missouri, Churchill coined the oft-quoted line, "Russia is a mystery, inside a riddle, wrapped in an enigma." In that same speech, he went on to say: "From what I have seen of our Russian friends, there is nothing for which they have more respect than strength and nothing for which they have less respect than weakness."

After reading my 1980 biography of Churchill, Nixon, in a note to me, underlined the famous "Russia is a riddle" line. He thus suggested that Churchill's insight into the psychology of Russia was more profound than the obvious conclusion that the Soviet Union respected only power.

The Soviet Union, in the 1970s, could not rival the United States in economic productivity. Its armies outnumbered America's, but in missile defense and nuclear power, it never achieved parity. Part of the fear it generated as the other world superpower was in its unpredictability. This uncertainty of the Kremlin's response to a U.S. initiative was an asset wielded extremely effectively by the Soviets during the Cold War.

In a conscious decision of statecraft, Nixon attempted to even the scales with the Soviet Union by floating the perception, through Kissinger's off-the-record talk to journalists and Russian diplomats, that "Nixon is a bit of a crazy man. . . . He can be something of a loose cannon."

This "unpredictability" that Nixon wanted to project to the Soviets was a direct application of the Sixth Commandment. Unpredictability, to Nixon, was not deliberate ambiguity or buttoned-up inscrutability. It was an unvoiced threat. Nixon aides in the National Security Council called it the "madman maneuver."

The Christmas bombing of 1972 was perhaps the culmination of this strategy. In a sense, it traces its beginnings back to 1968, to the "October surprise"—a term pols originally employed to describe a promise or initiative made in the closing weeks of a presidential campaign.

In 1968, Republican candidate Nixon expected President Johnson to announce some diplomatic breakthrough involving the Vietnam War. In Paris, former ambassador Harriman was meeting with the North Vietnamese. On October 31, President Johnson announced that North Vietnam had agreed to participate in peace talks, with the condition that the United States end all bombing north of the demilitarized zone. "I have now ordered," said the retiring president, Lyndon Johnson, "that all air, naval, and artillery bombardment of North Vietnam cease as of 8:00 A.M. Washington time, Friday morning [November 1]." That was the Democrats' "October surprise."

As a result, Vice President Humphrey took the lead in the polls. Then South Vietnam indicated it would not participate, and the prospect of peace talks collapsed. The night before the election, Nixon and Humphrey appeared in a mammoth telethon. (Both national parties had bought TV time to deliver a last-night-vote electional appeal whereby listeners could phone in questions.) After lamenting that the peace negotiations had collapsed, Nixon, in his own "surprise," reported that "the North Vietnamese are moving thousands of supplies down the Ho Chi Minh Trail, and our bombers are not able to stop them." (Aerial reconnaissance photographs later proved the validity of the Nixon claim.) The next day, Nixon defeated Humphrey in a very close election.

Despite the failure to achieve peace negotiations, the ban on the bombing in North Vietnam was not lifted. The new president made no comment on whether his administration would continue the ban. On behalf of North Vietnam, Soviet ambassador Dobrynin tried to find out from Secretary of State Rogers if the no-bombing commitment was still operative. Nixon would say nothing. He did not feel bound by the previous president's commitment to bring the North Vietnamese to a peace table that did not exist, but he did not take that position publicly. Although the United States did not resume its bombing of the North, Nixon remained noncommittal to those of his diplomatic adversaries who tried to pin him down. He now possessed the edge of unpredictability.

One factor that contributed to Nixon's victory in 1968 was that he had "a plan to end the war in Vietnam." Vaguely couched, the pledge could be accepted by both doves and hawks who could respectively interpret such a plan as either withdrawing U.S. troops or stepping up our involvement to achieve victory. Although Nixon's critics viewed the plan as a cynical campaign ploy, Nixon did have a plan—which he revealed only to intimates. It was to "Vietnamize" the war by gradually withdrawing U.S. troops.

During his early months at the White House, Nixon worked out a timetable for U.S. withdrawal and entered into direct negotiations with the North Vietnamese on political and military issues.

Since Ho Chi Minh believed that antiwar protests would force Nixon to pull out U.S. troops unilaterally, he was not interested in peace negotiations. To enter such talks would be to admit that the North Vietnam Army (NVA) was in South Vietnam, when they maintained the fiction that it was only the South Vietnamese people revolting against the Saigon government.

But, by the election year of 1972, North Vietnam was forced to reassess its opposition to peace negotiations for three reasons. First, Nixon's "triangular" diplomacy in quest of détente now meant that North Vietnam could no longer count on Beijing and Moscow for unqualified support. Only food and medical supplies were being shipped. The People's Republic's support of North Vietnam had always been more symbolic than substantive. China saw North Vietnam as a bit too close to Russia. Furthermore, the idea of a rapacious Vietnamese army absorbing Cambodia, Laos, and other countries on the peninsula was not looked on with any enthusiasm by the Chinese.

Secondly, the South Vietnam army's mining of Haiphong Harbor in the spring had halted the NVA offensive in its tracks. The south was reasserting itself.

And third, the North Vietnamese could read the U.S. polls, which indicated that Nixon would defeat McGovern by a landslide.

Nixon sent a warning to Hanoi that if the North Vietnamese rejected a peace offer when they met with Americans in Paris on October 8, Nixon would "turn to other methods" after the election.

On October 9, Kissinger responded from Paris: "Tell the President that there has been some definite progress at today's first session." Three days later, North Vietnam's chief negotiator, Le Duc Tho, who had previously stonewalled talks, unveiled a new peace plan: a cease-fire; the withdrawal of U.S. forces; the return of all prisoners of war on both sides; and no further infiltration of the South by the NVA or Viet Cong.

Kissinger was euphoric. He told Nixon that a settlement was possible before the November elections. Nixon's response, however, was cautious. He thought that making the election act as a timetable would weaken our bargaining position with the North Vietnamese. He also insisted that President Thieu of South Vietnam agree to any settlement. "It cannot be a shotgun wedding," Nixon warned.

Nixon's reluctance to force the settlement was bad politics but real statesmanship. He must have been tempted to override Thieu's protest and sign a cease-fire before the election. Both Kissinger from Saigon and Chairman Brezhnev from Moscow increased the pressure by going public with the story of the peace agreement. When Kissinger returned to Washington, he told reporters, "We believe peace is at hand."

Nixon was furious. It sounded uncannily like Chamberlain's "peace in our time" in 1938 in Munich. To Nixon, this announcement would weaken the U.S. leverage with the North Vietnamese and undermine the chances of securing President Thieu's cooperation. He was right. South Vietnam said it would not honor any peace agreement it had not signed, and the North Vietnamese refused to meet Kissinger again for negotiations.

Nixon extricated himself from this growing chaos by making a national TV broadcast on November 2, in which he seized the high ground of principle: "We are not going to allow an election deadline or any other kind of deadline to force us into an agreement which would only be a temporary truce and not a lasting peace."

A couple of days later, Nixon's massive victory—in which he carried forty-nine states—now strengthened his hand.

Nixon began to put negotiations back on track by securing South Vietnam's agreement to the settlement with this guarantee to President Thieu: "You have my absolute assurance that if Hanoi fails to abide by the terms of this agreement, it is my intention to take swift and retaliatory action."

But now the North Vietnamese reneged. The presidential victory did not surprise them. What did surprise them was that the Democratic-controlled Congress lost only a few seats. Surely they would force Nixon to accept peace on their terms.

As former British minister of defense Jonathan Aitken wrote in his biography *Nixon*, "Not for the first time, Hanoi underestimated Nixon." Nixon told his military advisers to prepare contingency plans for a bombing campaign in the North. At the same time, he gave Kissinger more flexible negotiating instructions to enable him to reach an agreement with Le Duc Tho. But the North Vietnam negotiator stonewalled and sidestepped the issues with an attitude of disdain. It was obvious that Le Duc Tho was negotiating in bad faith with no intention of reaching an agreement.

Back in Washington, Kissinger summed up the negotiations. "Mr. President," he said, banging his fist upon the table, "they're just a bunch of shits. Tawdry, filthy shits. They make the Russians look good compared to the way the Russians make the Chinese look good when it comes to negotiating in a responsible and decent way."

Nixon didn't have to be convinced of their perfidy. By using delaying tactics at the peace table, the North Vietnamese were trying to regain what they had lost through their military defeats on the battlefield.

Nixon, therefore, had to face up to what he called "the most difficult decision I made during the entire war—whether or not to direct a bombing attack on military targets in North Vietnam." Coincidentally, in this week before Christmas,

NIXON'S TEN COMMANDMENTS OF STATECRAFT

Nixon was reading *World Crisis,* Churchill's World War I memoirs, when he was struck by this observation: "One can have a policy of audacity or one can follow a policy of caution, but it is disastrous to try to follow a policy of audacity and caution at the same time."

"Audacity" would describe Nixon's eventual orders for what became known as the Christmas bombing. For the first time in the war, he sent large numbers of B-52s over the northern part of Vietnam in a sustained barrage.

During the period of December 18 to December 30 (with the exception of Christmas Day), he commanded up to 120 B-52 strikes a day against military objectives in the Hanoi-Haiphong area. Shipyards, power stations, armament plants, and military bases were destroyed.

When news of the bombing reached the United States, Nixon was attacked by the press. "War by Tantrum" (James Reston, *The New York Times*); "Shame on Earth" (Tom Wicker, *The New York Times*); "Acting Like a Maddened Tyrant" (Anthony Lewis, *The New York Times*). Senate Majority Leader Mike Mansfield described it as a "Stone Age tactic." Senator Ted Kennedy said, "It should outrage the conscience of all Americans." The Democratic Congressional leaders warned him that funds for continuing the war would be cut off.

In the firestorm, the left questioned the sanity of Nixon. Only a madman, they said, would "conduct indiscriminate bombing of civilian populations." Comparisons were made to Hiroshima.

Eventually, the real facts of the Christmas bombing replaced the hysteria. Only 1,300 were killed—mostly by falling debris from the 1,600 SAMs (surface-to-air missiles) fired against the American bombers. Far from destroying the peace talks, the bombing impelled them. The irony was that North Vietnamese intransigence ebbed as the rising tide of outrage from American liberal opinion soared. The North Vietnamese politburo sent instructions to the negotiating team in Paris: "Settle."

On the President's birthday, January 9, Le Duc Tho accepted the terms that Kissinger had proposed in November. Nixon still had a struggle to get President Thieu to sign on.

Nixon privately told Haig as he left for Saigon, "Brutality is nothing. You have never seen it if this son-of-a-bitch doesn't go along, believe me."

To Thieu, he wrote:

I have therefore irrevocably decided to proceed to initial the Agreement on January 23, 1973 and to sign it on January 27, 1973 in Paris. I will do so, if necessary, alone. In that case I shall have to explain publicly that your Government obstructs peace. The result will be an inevitable and immediate termination of U.S. economic and military assistance which cannot be forestalled by a change of personnel in your government. . . . We will react strongly in the event the agreement is violated. Finally, I want to emphasize my continued commitment to the freedom and progress of the Republic of Vietnam. It is my firm intention to continue full economic and military aid.

Thieu quibbled almost to the last day. He yielded on January 21.

To force the North Vietnamese to get serious at the negotiating table, Nixon had played the bombing card. Nixon never told the North Vietnamese that he would continue the ban on bombing that his predecessor had made. He would not tell them in advance what he would *not* do. When he did decide to bomb, it was to force North Vietnam to sign peace terms.

"Predictability" and "unpredictability" are both diplomatic

tools of statecraft. In defense, the unambiguous response to a possible attack is paramount. Truman's secretary of state, Dean Acheson, was a target of Senator Nixon's wrath in 1950 because of his ill-considered statement "South Korea is not within the perimeter of American defense"—words that might have invited Communist North Korea in their invasion in June 1950 across the thirty-eighth parallel.

On the other hand, unpredictability may be wielded as an unvoiced threat, as Nixon did, as long as the power to carry out that threat is readily apparent. Such a weapon in statecraft should not be forsworn without a compensatory concession from the adversary.

The business executive, in bargaining sessions, may well decide to lay the format for the "madman maneuver" or the "unpredictability ploy." If a buyer or seller believes the likelihood of an action such as seeking the services of another company, mounting a hostile takeover, or eliminating in terms of consolidation that particular phase of the business, he is more amenable to a deal. To reassure him beforehand that such measures are not being considered is to throw away a key tool, the "unpredictability" weapon.

Benjamin Disraeli

According to his daughter Julie, one of Nixon's favorite historical personalities was Benjamin Disraeli. Nixon had read and reread both the Blake and Pearson biographies, and although he did not have a taste for fiction, he had even perused the novel *Coningsby*, which Disraeli wrote before he became prime minister. Perhaps Nixon identified with the Jewish Disraeli as an outsider who rose to head the party of the Establishment—the Conservatives. Ironically, Nixon's chief foreign policy aide, Henry Kissinger, who was Jewish, looked to a German, Otto von Bismarck, as his historical model.

Prince Otto von Bismarck, the Iron Chancellor, is the leader most identified with the application of Realpolitik. Yet Nixon would remind Kissinger that the only one ever to out-maneuver Bismarck at the conference table was Disraeli. It was at the Congress of Berlin.

The German chancellor had called the conference in June 1878 to ratify accords on the current Balkan problem. The details had already been worked out months earlier, at the Treaty of San Stefano. The Congress of Berlin was only to be the venue where the European powers would formally sign their agreement. The treaty was the resolution of the Russo-Turkish War, in which Russian armies had defeated the Ottoman Empire. British prime minister Disraeli, however, was not happy with the tentative terms of San Stefano.

Disraeli now led the British government from the House of Lords. Queen Victoria had recently advanced him to the peerage by making him the earl of Beaconsfield. At the age of seventy-four, Disraeli suffered the complaints of the old: gout, rheumatism, and a bad heart, but the power of his mind had not diminished.

A year earlier, when Disraeli had sensed that Russia might invade Turkey, he extracted pledges from Czar Alexander II that Russia not encroach on three areas vital to the British Empire: the Suez Canal, the Dardanelles, and Constantinople. In the ensuing conflict, czarist armies had invaded the Ottoman Empire and set up a vassal Slav state of Bulgaria, and then entered Turkey to occupy the heights overlooking Constantinople. Strictly speaking, Russia had not technically violated the pledge: Constantinople, the Dardanelles, and Suez remained free. Nevertheless, their security was now in jeopardy.

The ailing Disraeli had not attended the San Stefano Conference at Constantinople but had sent in his place Lord Salisbury, the British foreign secretary. At that meeting, a victorious Russia had reluctantly accepted the terms pressed upon her by Bismarck, agreeing to disgorge some of the territory seized and occupied by her armies. Since Russia's principal ally, France, had agreed with the outline of the Bismarck plan, Russian negotiators felt they had no choice. Even though the troops of the Czar were still occupying most of Bulgaria right up to Constantinople, they were exhausted and too far from their home base to force better terms.

Russia could console itself that it had a satellite state of Bulgaria, which would provide access to the Mediterranean. Russia would also occupy major parts of Armenia, thus taking a stride toward India and closing in on Asiatic Turkey from the rear. Turkey lost all her European provinces.

Disraeli feared that Russia was now poised at the gate to the Middle East and remained a potential threat. He was not about to go to Berlin and sign away these advantages to Russia. He informed the czarist government that he would only attend if Russia gave up on its idea of a Great Bulgaria (a Russian puppet state) and a Russian Armenia.

The czarist ambassador took a carriage to 10 Downing Street. He raged at Disraeli, "My Lord, you are depriving Russia of all her fruits of war!" Disraeli remained adamant.

The Ambassador went away disturbed but doubtful. Would Disraeli really ask the cabinet to go to war to interfere with Russia's plans? Like Nixon, Disraeli was brandishing the unvoiced threat—Disraeli did not raise the idea of war, but he said nothing that foreclosed that option. Like Nixon, he used the "madman maneuver."

In the complicated power struggle for Europe, Bismarck was engaged in a constant balancing act to maintain German dominance. From its base of Prussia, he had forged a German empire. Bismarck's natural ally was Austria, a fellow German-speaking nation on its southern border. Austria's main adversary was Russia, which was seen to be stirring up the Slav minorities to rebel against the Austro-Hungarian Empire, and Russia's principal ally was France—the czarist court at St. Petersburg even spoke French. The close tie between Russia and France was a potential threat to Bismarck.

France, which had only recently lost Alsace-Lorraine to Germany, bridled at Bismarck's imperialism. At the preliminary conference at San Stefano, Bismarck had sided with Austria to pare the conquests of Russia. Yet if czarist Russia was to be stripped of all the fruits of its victory over Turkey, it might—with French backing—move into some of the Slav dependencies in the Austro-Hungarian Empire. Such a military encroachment would impel Bismarck to back Austria, thereby triggering a European war. For Bismarck, it was a balancing act—strip czarist Russia of some of its gains to satisfy its chief ally, Austria, but not so much that it would anger the Czar into provocative action involving France, Russia's main ally and Germany's chief adversary.

The preliminary arrangements at Constantinople—presided over by Bismarck—had left all the European powers relatively satisfied except for two on the fringe—the recently defeated Ottoman Turkish Empire, whose nation straddled Europe and Asia, and Britain, divided from continental Europe by the English Channel.

It was Disraeli's belief that the Russian demands on Turkey were excessive, for they practically amounted to the future domination of the Balkans by Russia and, even more dangerous to Britain, the creation of a strong Russian presence in the Straits of the Dardanelles.

Disraeli declared to the House of Lords, "If we are firm and determined, we shall have peace, and we shall dictate the terms for Europe." The Russians interpreted this as an ultimatum. Disraeli gave force to his words by calling up reserves, dispatching a fleet to Constantinople, and sending one battalion from India to Cyprus, in the eastern Mediterranean.

Russia, not wanting a war with England, backed down. Her military strength had been depleted by her recent war with Turkey, and furthermore, she virtually had no fleet. When Russia agreed to consider stepping back from the preliminary terms, Disraeli relented and accepted the invitation to Berlin.

The Earl of Beaconsfield arrived as the star of the Congress. Among the bouquets of flowers and baskets of strawberries that filled his suite, there was a note: "The Chancellor [Bismarck] would like to see Lord Beaconsfield as soon as possible." The two men had met in London some ten years before. Each had divined in the other an intelligence and fierce resolve.

The next day was the official opening of the Congress. Word circulated that Britain was not about to sign the worked-out settlement and had forced Russia to reconsider the price of the attendance of the British prime minister. Bismarck agreed to Disraeli's insistence that Russian troops withdraw from Bulgaria, but he demanded that Turkey also withdraw its armies. This did not satisfy Disraeli, who believed that Russia only had to move its troops across Bulgaria to reestablish it as a Russian satellite.

In Parliament before leaving, Disraeli had thundered his opposition to the plan: "Saint Petersburg must understand that the will of Britain will not be circumvented." Disraeli wrote Queen Victoria, "I shall break up this Congress if England's views are not adopted." Disraeli would insist on the Congress's acceptance of British policy on the Balkans: that Constantinople, eastern gateway to the Mediterranean, should not be closely menaced by a satellite of Russia's, a new Bulgaria. To prove his point, Disraeli chartered a special train to take him to Berlin. He would leave the train steaming in the Berlin depot as he awaited the agreement to British terms. The implication was that he was immediately ready to return to London and urge military action.

When Bismarck heard of the train that was steaming in the Berlin station, he called his carriage and went to see Disraeli at his suite at the Kaiserhof Hotel.

Bismarck asked Disraeli, "My Lord, am I to understand it as an ultimatum?"

"You presume correctly," replied Disraeli.

"We should talk this over," answered Bismarck. "Where will you dine today?"

"The British Embassy," responded Disraeli.

At the embassy dinner that night, Disraeli convinced the German chancellor that it was no bluff. Bismarck agreed to the British terms on Russia—that the czarist armies should withdraw from the Bulgar region.

Disraeli wrote to the Queen: "After dinner we retired to another room where he smoked cigars, and I followed his example. I believe I gave the last blow to my shattered constitution, but I felt it absolutely necessary. In such circumstances, the man who does not smoke has the appearance of spying on another's words. Before I went to bed, I had the satisfaction of knowing that Saint Petersburg had surrendered." When Disraeli got the telegram that the Czar had finally capitulated, he said to his aide, "What is the use of power if you don't make people do what they don't like?"

The Treaty of Berlin was signed on July 13, 1878. Bulgaria did not become a Russian "province" and Turkey retained the right to deploy troops in the Bulgar area. A feeble and ailing Disraeli was given medication by his doctor to allow him to attend the meeting and sign the document. Bismarck, who knew he had been outmaneuvered, said to an aide, "The Jew—there is a man!"

Then Disraeli left for London in the train, still waiting for him in the station. He arrived in London to say, "We have achieved peace with honour." The Queen made him Knight of the Garter.

Queen Victoria told him, "It is all due to your energy and firmness." Disraeli emitted a wry smile. "Sometimes you have to speak like Mars."

When Disraeli ordered the special train, he invited the inference that if Russia did not settle on Britain's terms, he would return to London and advise the Queen to declare war. Disraeli did not actually threaten war. He did not say that he *would* go to war, but neither did he say that he would *not*.

Russia did not underestimate Disraeli. It believed that the "madman" Disraeli might very well convince the Queen to take such a course.

In business, law, and diplomacy, implicit threats, with the apparent power to carry them off, are powerful leverage, because they make your adversary uneasy and unsure. Their uncertainty becomes an asset you can wield during negotiations. But there is little sense in using a threat or a challenge unless you are fairly sure the other side will believe you.

North Vietnam did not believe that Nixon would brook the opposition of the press and Democratic Congress and bomb the North, even though Nixon had specifically not ruled out that option. The Christmas Bombing ordered by Nixon made them believers.

On the other hand, Bismarck believed Disraeli. The risk of war impelled Bismarck to force the British policy down the Czar's throat.

VII

ALWAYS LEAVE YOUR ADVERSARY A
FACE-SAVING LINE OF RETREAT.

Nixon

Nixon's Seventh Commandment is much more than a maxim for magnanimity, a virtue for which his political foes give him scarce credit. Yet at the Nixon funeral, I heard Linda Johnson Robb say that of her mementos, she most treasured a handwritten letter that Nixon had sent to her son about his grandfather in 1974.

Similarly, I heard acts of kindness rendered to the members of the Kennedy family, such as inviting them to the private quarters of the White House. Nixon also called on the Senator's son, Teddy, when he had his leg amputated.

It is also not generally known that President-elect Nixon provided an official air force plane to take outgoing Vice President Humphrey back to Minnesota after his participation in Nixon's inaugural ceremonies in 1969. In January 1961, when Nixon was departing vice president, no one offered him a plane. He determined that Humphrey would at least be afforded a leave-taking with dignity.

Yet this commandment bespeaks no warm-hearted notions

of mercy but the cold self-interest of statecraft. On more than one occasion, Nixon quoted the words of Confucius, a minister of justice in China in the sixth century B.C.: "Build a golden bridge of escape for your enemies."

The advice of the Chinese philosopher-statesman suggests a much different theory than that of Machiavelli, who warned that if you go after a king you'd better kill him. The longer view of the wise Confucius appealed to Nixon. Today's enemy may be tomorrow's ally, and that possibility should never be foreclosed.

In the Yom Kippur War of October 1973, Nixon applied this precept toward Egyptian president Anwar Sadat. Sadat was an adversary because he, together with President Assad of Syria, had launched a war against Israel with the military backing of the Soviet Union. The initial advances by Egypt and Syria threatened the security of Israel, but when massive aid from the United States eventually arrived, the Israeli army had the capability for the total military destruction of Egypt.

In Moscow, the Soviets were alarmed at the direction the war in the Middle East was taking. By supplying planes, the Soviets had encouraged the twin-pronged advances of the Egyptian army across the Suez Canal and the Syrians across the Golan Heights. Now, the tide of the war had been reversed, and the Soviets, hoping to preserve some influence in the Arab world, pressed for an end of hostilities.

President Nixon dispatched his secretary of state, Henry Kissinger, to the Soviet Union to negotiate a cease-fire.

Although Nixon had come to the rescue of Israel with a massive air supply of weaponry, he still worried about the consequences of a crushing defeat on Egypt's Anwar Sadat. As an obscure army officer, Sadat helped General Gamal Abdel Nasser plan the coup that ousted the corrupt regime of King Farouk in 1952. The handsome and charismatic Nasser became the idol of the Arab world. His death in 1970 would spark one of the greatest outpourings of grief the world had ever seen. His quiet, self-effacing lieutenant, Anwar Sadat, then succeeded him.

Nixon first took note of Sadat when he met Nasser in 1963. Though he was derided by some as "Nasser's poodle," Nixon sensed an assurance and dignity in Nasser's chief of staff.

His initial impression was justified when Sadat, upon becoming president, quickly acted to break the fetters that bound Egypt to the Soviets. In 1972, he abruptly expelled sixteen thousand Soviet military advisers. Sadat found the Russians not only unreliable but unmannered. In 1974, he would confide to Nixon, "We Egyptians are more civilized than the Russians."

Nixon perceived the contrasts between Nasser and his successor. Nixon would later write, "Sadat was as practical as Nasser was flighty, as careful as Nasser was impulsive." In short, if Nasser was the romanticist, Sadat was that rare specimen in the Arab Middle East—a realist. Yet the viability of any political future for Sadat was now jeopardized. The Israeli army had surrounded Egypt's twenty-five-thousand-man Third Army Corps. Its demise would spell the destruction of Sadat.

The Third Army was the pride of the Egyptian forces, boasting the professional elite of their military. At the beginning of the invasion on October 7, 1973, the Egyptian army had crossed the southern end of the Suez Canal and gained a foothold about ten miles wide and thirty miles long in the Israeli-occupied Sinai Peninsula, which Egypt had lost to Israel in the 1967 war.

But in a daring move, the Israeli army, led by General Sharon, crossed the canal—north of the Third Army—and then moved southward to cut it off from the rest of the Egyptian forces. The Israelis were close to capturing the Third Army's last supply link—the Cairo-Suez highway—just as the in-place cease-fire was about to commence.

The Israelis were not happy with the terms of the cease-fire. Not only would they lose the chance to annihilate Egypt as a potential military threat, but they would also have to give up the gains in the Sinai they secured in the Six-Day War six years earlier.

Only by offering Israeli prime minister Golda Meir a loophole did Kissinger secure her consent to the cease-fire "in place." In Tel Aviv, the Israelis asked to defer immediate compliance with the cease-fire resolution—now endorsed by the United Nations. Meir's argument was that "in the Vietnam agreements with the U.S. the previous year, the cease-fire did not go into effect at the exact time it was agreed on."

With that indirect go-ahead, the Israelis disregarded the cease-fire and moved to complete their destruction of the Third Army. Prime Minister Golda Meir clothed their assault in the thin claim that Israel was only responding to provocation.

Nixon leaned on Israel to cease its attack. Israel agreed to hold its guns from firing but refused to let Egyptian convoys pass carrying food, water, and medical supplies to the Third Army. Desperate, President Sadat now appealed to President Nixon for an airlift—a plea full of irony since the United States had weeks before assisted its adversary, Israel, with air shipments.

Nixon did not answer Sadat's request, but he did deliver a stern protest to Israel. "We cannot permit the destruction of the Egyptian army under conditions achieved after a cease-fire was reached, in part by negotiations in which we participated." If the Israeli army did not permit the resupply of nonmilitary items to the Egyptian Third Army, Nixon brandished the threat of ultimate abandonment: Soviet airborne forces were prepared to intervene directly to save the Egyptian armies. Unless Israel accepted the cease-fire, the United States would not stand in the way of the Soviet Union.

Sadat then offered to engage in direct Egyptian-Israeli military talks in order to resolve the problem of supply to his Third Army along the Cairo-Suez road. All the Egyptian president asked was that one convoy be allowed through the military cordon to keep his men alive. Israel consented. The medical convoy was waved through by Israeli troops.

In the predawn hours of Sunday, October 28, at a marker designating kilometer 101 on the road from Cairo to Suez, Egypt's Lieutenant General Abdel Gamasy and Israel's Major General Sharon Yarov nervously approached each other. They exchanged awkward salutes and then shook hands. Kilometer 101 was destined to become a milestone in history. As foreign policy commentator Edward Sheehan wrote, "This was the food of history." The encounter was the first face-to-face talk between Israel and Arab representatives in the quarter of a century since the state of Israel gained its independence in 1948.

Nixon believed that Sadat represented a future voice for moderation and restraint in the volatile Middle East. He prevented Israel from annihilating Sadat's army in order to preserve his leadership and thus the hope of a constructive peace settlement at a later time. For Sadat, the preservation of his army was a "face-saving line of retreat." But for the world, it was the foundation for the Egyptian-Israeli accord a few years later.

The term "scorched earth" was coined by General John Sullivan to describe the burning of Iroquois settlements in the Revolutionary War and was perfected by William Sherman in Georgia during the Civil War. That kind of total destruction may speed victory but impedes lasting peace after the victory. Short-term military tactics are often counterproductive to diplomatic strategy. The punitive Versailles Treaty after World War I is testament to that. If Germany had been left with some semblance of dignity, Hitler might never have emerged.

Lawyers should remember this face-saving advice when they write divorce settlements that make a father more likely to default on his obligations to his children, and business executives in a corporate takeover should remember that the callous treatment of the old company's executives by the new executives may endanger the loyalty of established clients. Magnanimity in management, whether in the executive suite or in the White House, is good business and good government.

Douglas MacArthur

Richard Nixon first saw Douglas MacArthur in 1951 when the general delivered his "Old Soldiers Never Die" address to the Joint Session of Congress. He first spoke to him when they both attended Senator Robert Taft's funeral in June 1953.

Nixon's admiration for the general had not always been unrestrained. As a junior naval officer in the Pacific, Nixon shared the navy man's resentment of the flamboyant and egotistical army commander of the Pacific. But when Nixon visited Japan as vice president in the fall of 1953, his respect for MacArthur approached awe as he surveyed the thriving postwar Japan that MacArthur's statesmanship had built.

Nixon was amazed to discover that MacArthur was the most esteemed man in Japanese society. MacArthur, whose formative years were spent in Asia and who had thoroughly studied the history of that continent, understood the Far East as few western politicians ever had. The Confucian precept, "Build a golden bridge of escape for your enemies," was surely a familiar maxim to him.

The Japanese people's respect for General MacArthur began when he arrived at Atsagi Airport from Manila on August 30, 1945. At the end of the war, President Truman had appointed MacArthur the Supreme Allied Commander for the Allied powers in Japan. In his biography of the general, William Manchester describes what an astonishing spectacle it was for "an unarmed five-star general to drop out of the sky into the midst of a nation of seventy million, who until weeks ago, had been pledged to its annihilation." When MacArthur noticed the others in the arrival party strapping on their guns, he said, "Take them off. If they intend to kill us, sidearms will be useless, and nothing will impress them like a show of absolute fearlessness."

Later, Churchill wrote of MacArthur's entry into Japan: "Of all the amazing deeds in the war, I regard General MacArthur's personal conduct at Atsagi Airport the bravest of the lot."

From Yokohama to Tokyo, MacArthur rode in an old Lincoln. Thirty thousand Japanese infantrymen lined the road, bayonets fixed. At the Tokyo Hotel, the owner showed MacArthur to his room. When he and his entourage were served steak for dinner, an aide tried to test it first in case of poison. MacArthur quickly took the steak away from him, laughing. "I'm not sharing that splendid steak with anyone." That story of MacArthur's respect for the Japanese honor of a host quickly made its rounds in Tokyo.

At the time of MacArthur's arrival, the secretary of treasury, Henry Morgenthau, who had drawn up a plan to lay economic waste to Germany, had a similar primitive blueprint for Japan. Surely MacArthur, who had been humiliated by the Japanese in Corregidor, would be receptive. MacArthur was not. The victorious general wanted not revenge, but rather, reconciliation. As he later wrote, he saw himself as "an economist, a political scientist, an engineer, a manufacturing executive, a teacher, and a theologian of sanity." MacArthur was determined that his achievements as proconsul would eclipse those on the battlefield.

The State Department and much of the United States academic community were insistent that the Japanese constitution of monarchy and parliament be scrapped and replaced by a model derived from the American presidential system.

MacArthur wanted to preserve the structure while rearranging some of the furniture. He understood the importance of "face" in Asia. His plan was to retain the Emperor and let the Japanese disarm themselves. He also refused to ban fraternization of American soldiers with Japanese women and threatened court-martial for any G.I. who bullied or struck a Japanese citizen.

U.S. liberals, some of whom called for the execution of Hirohito for war crimes, attacked MacArthur for being soft. I. F. Stone wrote in the *New Republic*, "It takes little reflection to realize that we can hardly hope to break the power of Japan's ruling classes—the aristocracy, the plutocracy, the bureaucracy, and the military—if we confine ourselves to operating through a government which remains their instrument."

The autocratic MacArthur was never popular with liberals. Yet the very qualities that they despised in MacArthur were admired by the Japanese: magisterial dignity; an air of remoteness; magniloquence of speech.

In manifesting an imperial presence, MacArthur was, after all, replacing the emperor as the real leader of Japan. Yet in his dealings with Hirohito, MacArthur was a model of courtly manners and exquisite tact. In his first meeting with the Emperor, MacArthur took no aide with him and afterward revealed nothing of the conversation to the press. MacArthur told an aide, "Every honor due a sovereign was to be his."

Later, in his *Reminiscences*, MacArthur wrote that Hirohito was "nervous." "I offered him a cigarette . . . his hands shook as I lighted it for him." Hirohito was aware that he was number one on the British and Russian war criminals execution list. Hirohito stoically accepted that fate and offered himself up to take the blame of the war.

MacArthur knew that Hirohito was more pawn than player in the Axis war cabinet's schemes for conquest. He was convinced that if Hirohito remained as emperor in a constitutional monarchy, the Japanese would be docile.

MacArthur saw little of Japan besides the embassy, his office at Dai Ichi, and the route connecting the two places. By withdrawing his presence, he enhanced his mystique of the unseen ruler.

In his office, MacArthur closeted himself to orchestrate the economic rebuilding phases of Japan. He broke up the old Japanese industrial combine by passing stiff tax laws. He also limited the profit foreign traders could take out of the country and approved the formation of labor unions. Colonel Robert McCormick of the right-wing *Chicago Tribune* labeled MacArthur's moves "socialistic economic policy." MacArthur answered, "This is not socialism, but it would be better to have real socialism than the association of monopolies."

In his very first week in Japan, MacArthur dispatched 3.5 million tons of food supplies the United States army had accrued in the Pacific area. The effect upon the Japanese was electric. Still, the House Appropriations Committee asked how MacArthur could justify the expenditure of army supplies to feed the enemy.

As MacArthur later wrote, "We fed the Japanese, but we didn't intend to feed them forever." MacArthur issued directives to rebuild factories, get the trains running, and renew overseas trade.

A tangled financial mess had to be unsnarled and a healthy economy put back in place. When MacArthur left in 1951,

Japan had enjoyed five years of a balanced budget and a relatively small public debt. For a country whose economy had been flattened to the ground, it was the most prosperous nation in Asia.

MacArthur also drafted a new Japanese constitution. The Emperor was reduced to a symbol, and the Diet (the assembly) was empowered to make laws. The feudal industry was abolished, and civil rights were guaranteed.

About a decade later, the General addressed the Ends of the Earth, the oldest Anglo-military organization, at the Union Club in New York. No reporters were allowed into this stag dinner. As president of the group for the last fifteen years, I have pieced his speech together by talking to those who were present:

> I will not liken myself to the great captains of antiquity, Alexander, Caesar, Napoleon, Wellington, who make my own achievements pale in comparison. But by one criterion, my record will invite favorable comparison to any commander of the past. Tacitus wrote, "Let the conquered judge the conqueror."
>
> I am content if the orphan or widow whose father or husband I had slain writes the judgment of Douglas MacArthur. There are those who call me a militarist, but no government charter anywhere ever forbade the right to bear arms until I had it put in the constitution.
>
> There are those who call me a reactionary, but there was no land reform ever enacted in Asia until I had it implemented in Japan.
>
> There are those who would label me a feudalist in my thinking, but no woman had the right to vote or own property until I enfranchised them in the Japanese constitution. "Let the conquered judge the conqueror."

MacArthur had ample reason to take pride. No proconsul in history had ever registered such a benign impact upon a country: popular liberties, land reform, women's suffrage, and collective bargaining. His critics questioned not his ends but his means. MacArthur operated as a benevolent dictator—outside the reach of the Far Eastern Commission that included the British, French, and Russians, all with veto power.

The ratification of the new Japanese constitution in April 1946 did not please the Far Eastern Commission, which disapproved of the swiftness with which MacArthur was freeing defeated Japan. Few could have guessed how well the MacArthur constitution would stand the test of time. More than fifty years later, the loser, Japan, and victor, America, are the leading economic giants of the world. Yet, as MacArthur noted in his *Reminiscences*, "The economic miracle of Japan would not have happened if left to the devices of the Far Eastern Commission, which had the Soviet veto to contend with."

Offering a defeated adversary a way to save face can be good statecraft. It lances the rancor that could lead to a virulent nationalism. By face-saving, MacArthur, with his proconsulship in Japan, paved the way for a nation without a tradition of freedom to develop a democracy.

Face-saving also makes sense in law and business. A business executive, when he dismisses a major employee, wants to make sure he does not return bearing a grudge in the company of a competitor or a major customer. The law partner who is squeezed out may become general counsel of a major client of his former firm and could steer business away.

Today, outplacement efforts by downsizing companies are proof of the principle. The growth industry of employment agencies specializing in counseling, referral, and placement is a result of businesses realizing the wisdom of treating bested adversaries with grace and dignity.

As Chester Karrass wrote in *Give and Take*, "Face-saving is

VIII

ALWAYS CAREFULLY DISTINGUISH
BETWEEN FRIENDS WHO PROVIDE
SOME HUMAN RIGHTS AND ENEMIES
WHO DENY ALL HUMAN RIGHTS.

Nixon

Nixon's Eighth Commandment might offend the moral absolutists in foreign policy. Yet Nixon was a Quaker whose first hero of foreign policy was Woodrow Wilson. He respected the position of idealists in international affairs, even though he thought their views often impractical in the realities of Cold War politics.

What Nixon disdained was the double standard of his liberal critics who waxed indignant at the human rights violations of our allies but turned a blind eye toward the totalitarian brutalities of our enemies.

Nixon's precept is not a euphemistic variation of "The end justifies the means," for he is not asserting that any repression by our friends should be overlooked. He is not advocating condonation of the violations of human rights, but rather that any denial of rights be judged in context.

Dr. Jeane Kirkpatrick of Georgetown University won the attention of presidential candidate Ronald Reagan in 1979 for her academic treatise differentiating between "authoritarians" and "totalitarians." By her definition, an authoritarian government was defined as a regime that offered some freedoms even though it was a one-party monopoly with a nonelected head of state. Some freedoms included a free press, freedom of assembly, uncontrolled academic freedom in the universities, an independent judiciary, and a free market. At least two of these freedoms—along with the fact that they were allies of the United States—made them authoritarian. Although a liberal, Democrat Kirkpatrick had been a foreign affairs adviser for Hubert Humphrey, and her views were attacked by many as reactionary. Authoritarian, to Kirkpatrick's critics, described any right-wing dictator who allied himself with U.S. foreign policy objectives. The left found any military or economic assistance to such countries—South Vietnam, Korea, Taiwan, Pakistan, or Iran, for instance—unjustifiable and immoral.

While Nixon did not disagree with Dr. Kirkpatrick's terminology, he counseled that first, we should make a comparison between the leader of a friendly country and the alternative. Examples included South Vietnam and North Vietnam, South Korea and North Korea, Iran (under the Shah) and Iraq. Would Ho Chi Minh's Communist regime be as "democratic" as the government of President Thieu, which tolerated free elections, religious freedom, and the right of opposition journals to operate? Would the North Korean psychopath Sung offer a more open society than President Park?

Second, Nixon was implicitly arguing that a free market economy, which both South Vietnam and South Korea were encouraging, was a basic freedom totalitarian Marxism did not recognize. It was Nixon's belief that economic liberty, even if under autocratic governments, generated mounting pressure to open up society. In other words, if economic freedom comes, it is usually soon followed by political freedom. Nixon would cite Chile, Taiwan, and Singapore, as well as South Korea, as evidence.

Nixon always thought it risky to meddle in the internal affairs of any nation, but to coerce our allies, who were already moving toward a more open society, was unthinkable.

The contrasting treatment of the Shah of Iran by the Nixon and Carter administrations offers a case study in this dilemma. In 1976, Democratic presidential candidate Carter made human rights a centerpiece of his election campaign. His speeches condemned previous administrations' tolerance of repressive governments in pursuit of its foreign policy objectives. He criticized Nixon's Realpolitik as an immoral betrayal of the Declaration of Independence ideals. The Nixon policy in Iran, he charged, had been sacrificing American principles of human liberty on the altar of petroleum.

It is certainly true that access to Iranian oil was a factor in the friendship between the two nations. Oil, however, is not opium or even tobacco. It is a staple of the modern economy more important than bread. Oil enables Americans to heat their homes and drive to work, farmers to plow their fields, and ambulances to carry the sick and injured to the hospital. If oil becomes scarce and its price rises, the economy is stifled and unemployment mounts. The elderly and impoverished suffer in chilly apartments and are more vulnerable to disease and death.

Just as critical as its oil was Iran's steadying influence in the volatile politics of the Middle East. Iran was both the most economically developed and the least fanatic of the Islam nations in the Middle East. Unlike other Muslim countries, it maintained working (if not warm) ties with Israel. Indeed, the two Middle Eastern countries had long been trading partners despite their religious differences.

Critics of the close ties between the Nixon administration and the Iranian regime decried the imperial splendor of the Peacock Throne and the brutality of SAVAK (the Iranian secret police). Yet, as David Lamb writes in *The Arabs: Beyond the Mirage,* the pharaonic opulence of Sadat in Cairo rivaled the Shah's monarchical magnificence in Tehran.

True, the Shah's regime was authoritarian, but again, only marginally more than Sadat's tight grip on freedoms in Egypt. It was a royal kingdom similar to that of King Faisal of Saudi Arabia and King Hussein of Jordan. All three of these monarchs daily faced the threat of assassination by radical Islamic fanatics. King Faisal would be assassinated in 1975 and President Sadat in 1981. It is not surprising that heads of state in Muslim nations would rely on brutal security police. Indeed, the Shah, who had displaced the theocratic power of the mullahs, was an even more hated target for radical Islamic sects.

What made the Shah unpopular with many Iranians was not so much the excesses of his secret police as the reforms he had instituted to modernize Iran. He had angered the big land-owning aristocracy by breaking up the estates for small farmers and antagonized the industrialists by requiring them to sell shares of their corporations to the public. He had enraged the Iranian merchants by passing laws that made the exorbitant profiteering of middlemen a crime.

Finally, he infuriated the Islamic priesthood by enfranchising women with civil rights. Women were now "equal partners" with men—in matters of divorce and property rights. Even more objectionable was his decree that the Iranian government would be secular—separate from the Islamic faith.

The endeavor to force Iran from the religious foundation of its past brought the Shah many enemies. Both reactionary and radical elements viewed him as a tool of the United States. The Shah, it is true, had openly linked himself to the United States.

In May 1972, on his way back from Moscow, President Nixon stopped for a day in Tehran to visit the Shah. Nixon asked the Shah to defend the U.S. interests in the Persian Gulf. These American concerns included military and political support of U.S. allies such as Saudi Arabia, Jordan, and the emirates. Britain, once a colonial power in the Middle East, had withdrawn from "east of the Suez" and could no longer be looked to for assistance.

In the Nixon Doctrine announced at Guam in 1969, the President had explained that the United States would no longer commit troops to assist beleaguered allies. Nixon said to the Shah, "Protect us." And indeed, he did.

As Henry Kissinger later wrote:

> Iran's influence was always on our side; its resources reinforced ours even in some distant enterprises—in aiding South Vietnam at the time of the 1973 Paris Agreement; helping western Europe in its economic crisis in the 1970's; supporting moderation in Africa against Soviet-Europe encroachment; supporting President Sadat in the later Mideast diplomacy. In the Middle East War, Iran was the *only* country bordering the Soviet Union not to permit the Soviet use of their airspace—in contrast to several national allies.

The Shah took on the brunt of attention from his radical Arab neighbors, such as Syria and Iraq, and deflected their threats to the moderate regimes in Saudi Arabia, Jordan, and the emirates. He refueled U.S. fleets and never joined any embargo against the West or Israel.

In 1976, however, Jimmy Carter, the Democratic presidential candidate, denounced our relationship with the Shah as a bargain with the devil. He attacked the Kissinger foreign policy of selling Iran—a dictatorial regime—F-14 and F-15 fighter equipment. Omitted was the fact that Iran could easily have purchased the only slightly less advanced Mirage planes from France.

Carter chose to make human rights the centerpiece of his

political crusade, and the nation that was his case example was Iran. Nowhere in his speeches did Carter mention gulags in Russia, prison torture in Cuba, or the totalitarian brutality in North Korea. In other words, Carter was applying a double standard—one for our allies and another for our adversaries.

For the Shah, Carter's rhetoric was chilling. His rejection of the Nixon and Ford practice of selling arms to Iran was further proof to the Shah that Carter was trying to topple the Peacock Throne.

The Shah's enemies in Iran rejoiced at Carter's victory in 1976. As the British ambassador to Iran reported, "They took comfort and refuge from what they rightly perceived as the weakening of the absolute support which the Shah had received from Washington for so many years." That perception emboldened the Shah's opponents. Jimmy Carter cast doubt on the U.S. commitment to the Shah, while simultaneously encouraging his opposition. On May 19, 1977, the new president outlined his foreign policy strategy and denounced "the inordinate fear of Communism by the United States." Carter said, "The old policy led America to embrace any dictator who opposed Communism."

The Shah got the message. He sought an invitation to visit Carter. He came to the United States in November and was greeted by anti-Shah demonstrations around the White House. Back in Iran, the Shah began to respond to opposition protests and demands. He let the exiled Ayatollah Khomeini return from France. The appeasement only stimulated the passion of the Shah's internal foes. Riots orchestrated by the Ayatollah multiplied in the first two years of the new U.S. administration. Even more damaging than the riots were the strikes. The lower-middle class galvanized in its violent opposition to the regime. With its firm control of the enormous government bureaucracy, this class's strikes paralyzed the nation.

On January 16, 1979, the Shah, broken in health and spirit,

left Tehran by plane. The Ayatollah Khomeini had replaced the royal regime with a theocratic dictatorship far harsher in its denial of human rights than its predecessor. On November 4, 1979, students "in the cause of Islam" crashed the doors of the U.S. Embassy, and the Iranian hostage crisis of the U.S. diplomats began.

Henry Kissinger, in his memoirs, asked a question: "Was it wrong for us to support one of our most valuable allies in 1972, or was it wrong to fail to support him in 1978 and 1979?"

By reneging on our commitment to a loyal friend, Carter created one of the most virulently anti-American nations in the world. The result did not help the Iranian people but pushed them back into a theocratic terrorism. What had been the most economically advanced nation in the Islamic world had now retrogressed into feudal poverty.

Punishing our friends never pays dividends in business or world affairs. The result is losses—a loss in influence, a loss in trade—losses that undermine a customer or ally. Carter's policy toward Iran not only destroyed a loyal friend in the Shah but diminished the prestige and influence of America. As Nixon once told me, "To take a magnifying glass to the faults of our friends and turn a blind eye to the record of our foes is not only wrong but stupid."

Sir Anthony Eden

Nixon once told me that when he was at Duke Law School in 1936, the English politician that most caught the students' fancies was not Churchill but Anthony Eden, the glamorous young British foreign secretary. The sixty-two-year-old Churchill was then assigned to the back benches, but the thirty-nine-year-old Eden, the head of the British Foreign Office, gained the spotlight as the principled advocate of the

League of Nations supporting Ethiopia against Mussolini's Italy. His posture struck a chord of idealism with the young law students. His matinee idol looks certainly did not diminish his appeal.

In the aftermath of World War I, the various European victors—Britain, France, and Italy—established footholds in many of the countries freed from the Ottoman Empire. Britain, for example, had protectorates or mandates in Palestine, Jordan, and Iraq; France in Syria; and Italy in Somaliland, which lay on Ethiopia's western border.

In 1922, the onetime journalist Benito Mussolini assumed power in Italy. He and his Fascist Party had gained several million adherents. The party possessed a powerful private army, and had won financial support from the bankers and industrialists.

Italy prospered for the rest of the booming 1920s, and Mussolini boasted of the success of his Fascist government. But the worldwide depression of 1929 struck Italy even harder than Britain and France because of Mussolini's dependence on a vast public works program. Italian exports plummeted, the Italian treasury went bankrupt, and there was a run on the lira. By 1934, unemployment was higher in Italy than in Britain or even Germany, and few of the unemployed drew any relief. Such economic failure at home impelled Il Duce to seek some triumph or victory abroad. Ethiopia was the most likely place to rekindle dreams of the imperial glory that once was Rome's.

On a December afternoon in 1934, two shots were fired on the edge of Walwal—the border area of watering holes that had been used by both Somali and Ethiopian nomadic tribesmen for centuries. Walwal, which means "wells" in Amharic, is not a town, but a vast oasis watered by a hundred springs. It lies in the Ogaden Plateau, a range that stretches some eight hundred miles from the Gulf of Aden south to Kenya.

The first shot was fired by a Somali soldier in a force led by an Italian captain, and it led to pitched battle between the Ethiopians and Italian-Somali forces. The Ethiopians, with over a hundred dead, withdrew from Walwal.

The Italian government had long been planning action against Ethiopia for reasons that had nothing to do with the Italian garrison at Walwal. But the incident presented a convenient pretext for invasion. The fact that Ethiopia presented no threat to Italy did not matter. What counted was that it was the last habitable portion of the world's surface still available for colonial expansion and that it adjoined its colony of Somaliland.

On December 14, 1934, the Ethiopians submitted the Walwal incident to the League of Nations in Geneva, claiming that an Italian invasion "threatens to disturb international peace."

The League of Nations was far more of an elite club than today's United Nations with its more than 180 members. Most of the countries were from Europe and Latin America. The United States was the one major nation that had refused to join. Asia was represented by only China and Japan. The sole African member was Ethiopia, which ironically had been sponsored by Italy in 1923.

Generally, the League, whose headquarters were in Switzerland, was dominated by Europe, and the key players were France and Britain, whose premiers were, respectively, Pierre Laval and Stanley Baldwin. Laval was a small, chain-smoking cynic who had only one foreign policy objective: to keep Fascist Italy from teaming up with Nazi Germany. For him, this matter of Ethiopia was a nuisance that could drive a wedge between France and its southeast neighbor.

For the bluff, pipe-smoking Yorkshireman Stanley Baldwin, all foreign policy, including the League, was a distraction. Baldwin, whom Churchill described as "having his ears so close to the ground that they were full of locusts," only knew one thing about international affairs—that the English people did not want any action that risked war.

In splendid contrast was Anthony Eden, whose youth and strikingly handsome features seemed to embody the idealism of a League of Nations still in its infancy. Eden believed that a League of Nations sanction against Italy in Ethiopia might establish a precedent against a rapacious Nazi Germany.

By virtue of breeding, brains, and good looks, Eden seemed early to be marked by the gods for leadership. The third son of Sir William Eden prepped at Eton. In 1914, at age seventeen, he enlisted in World War I. At the end of the war, he was, at age twenty, the nation's youngest major—an advancement no doubt speeded by his being awarded the Military Cross for bravery under fire.

After the war, Eden resumed his studies at Oxford, where he won a first-class degree in Oriental Studies. Though that course was often a stepping-stone to the Foreign or Colonial Office, Eden stood for Parliament in 1922. He lost, but in 1923, he won as a Conservative Member for Leamington and Warwick. As a young member, he was a Parliamentary secretary to Sir Austen Chamberlain, and then foreign secretary under Stanley Baldwin.

It was in that post that Eden first traveled to Geneva to observe the formal machinery of the League of Nations. He made this note on his first trip: "The experiment might have appeared hazardous, but it aroused brave hopes for me also. It seemed an opportunity to escape from a balance of power which had failed to keep the peace, to an international authority which might have had the collective strength to do so."

In 1931, Eden, at thirty-four, was appointed Minister of State for Foreign Affairs, the number two job in the British Foreign Office. The next year, Prime Minister Baldwin decided that a permanent British presence was needed at

Geneva. Eden was the instant choice. Two years later, in December 1934, after Eden was edged out of his deputy position in the Foreign Office, Baldwin—to placate the growing faction of Eden's supporters in the Conservative Party—made him Minister of State for the League of Nations. Along with this newly created ministry, Eden was also given the coveted honorific Lord Privy Seal to enhance his voice in international affairs.

So it was the thirty-seven-year-old Eden, as British minister, who heard Ethiopia's case against Italian aggression at the Walwal oasis. Eden dryly recorded his first reaction: "It is hard to believe that Italian ambitions are limited to a few wells."

His view was strengthened by both the Italian government's refusal to negotiate the border incident with Ethiopia and the appointment of General deBono to be the new high commissioner for Somaliland. The Italian press speculated that deBono was preparing a base for military operations for Italy's "civilizing mission" in Ethiopia.

In July 1935, Eden told the cabinet that an Italian invasion would violate the covenant of the League of Nations. Ignoring this covenant would deal a heavy blow to the system of pacts and agreements on which the postwar system of Europe had been built. Eden also reminded the cabinet that Ethiopia, since the days the Suez was built, had been historically a British ally.

Under pressure from Eden and the British government, Italy relented and agreed to subject the Walwal incident to arbitration. Eden was well aware that a tentative agreement to submit to future arbitration would not stop Mussolini from invading. So, on August 4, in a speech to England on the BBC from Geneva, Eden imposed a one-month deadline. The Italian press attacked this speech as an ultimatum for war.

Premier Laval then became skittish over Italian criticism. For him, some border dispute in remote East Africa was negligible compared with an armed Germany on France's northern border, when Hitler was threatening to occupy the Rhineland in violation of the Treaty of Versailles. Laval wanted to preserve France's military alliance with Italy at all costs. He advised the British to reduce their forces in the Mediterranean in order to ease tension with Italy.

In response, Eden told the British Cabinet: "It would be fatal in any way to reduce pressure on Signor Mussolini. Laval's game in the League is not to antagonize Italy while keeping alive the League for another cause [i.e., Germany] when it may be of value to them."

Meanwhile, Mussolini was rolling out his propaganda machine to blacken the name of Haile Selassie, the Emperor of Ethiopia, and his savage and barbarous African regime, which needed "the civilizing influence of a Christian nation." In fact, the Coptic nation of Ethiopia was Christian centuries before Rome, and Ethiopians lived in freedom, unlike the Italians, who were being governed by spies and bullies. True, Selassie had autocratic powers, but he allowed a free press and assembly. His monarchical descent extended back to King Solomon, while the House of Savoy had ruled Italy only since the nineteenth century.

Mussolini instructed journalists to distribute pictures of Amharic tribesmen in their native ceremonial garb, along with detailed descriptions and pictures of beheading (as in most Middle Eastern countries today, decapitation is the punishment for murder) and the unspeakable brutality of Ethiopian prisons.

In April 1970, when my wife and I were guests of the Earl and Countess of Avon in their home in Wiltshire, England (Eden was advanced to the peerage in 1961), Eden recalled the situation: "The Italians trumpeted the savagery of Ethiopians while they used poison gas in their fight against the Ethiopian army, and that was barbarity.

"Some of our press—including some who should have known better, like Evelyn Waugh—wrote about the corruption, squalor, and lack of hygiene in Addis Ababa.

"Many in France and here in England believed it because they wanted to. They would look for any excuse to justify *not* taking action against Mussolini."

On September 4, 1935, the Italian delegate at the League, Baron Aloisi, recited a litany of horrors about the Selassie regime. A few days later, Mussolini's son-in-law Count Ciano told an American audience that negotiation with Ethiopia or any arbitration was "a closed matter." The next day, when Hitler greeted the new Italian ambassador in Berlin, he talked of "a community of interest between Germany and Italy." Then, on September 10, Mussolini issued a massive mobilization order—a one-day "general assembly of the forces of the regime." The invasion of Ethiopia would take place on October 3, 1935.

The League, however, took no action for fear of triggering a European war. As Mussolini's armies moved across the border, Eden wrote to his constituents:

> The issues of the dispute are such as must profoundly interest every one of us. It is not purely a question of colonial adventure of no real importance, as has been urged in some quarters. It is not a question of the imperialist demand of one Power or another Power in the territory of Abyssinia or elsewhere. It is not even just a question of peace or war in an outlying part of the world. The real issue is whether or not the League of Nations can prove itself an effective instrument in this dispute, and whether its members are prepared to respect and uphold the Covenant. . . . The present dispute is a text case. [underscoring in original]

On October 9, as the League met, Eden called for sanctions—specifically an economic embargo against Italy: "Since it is our duty to take action, it is essential that such action should be prompt. That is the League's responsibility—a responsibility based on humanity: for we cannot forget that war is at this moment actually in progress."

His recommendations passed. It was a high point in the brief history of the League of Nations. Unfortunately, France, worried about alienating Italy, would later work to undo the sanctions when Germany invaded the Rhineland.

In June 1936, Britain's chancellor of the exchequer, Neville Chamberlain, attacked his fellow Conservative Eden, calling the sanctions as framed "the very midsummer of madness." A majority of the nations in the League, worried about the prospect of European war, agreed with Chamberlain's opinion. Sanctions were lifted.

Ever since the Suez Canal was finished in 1869, the British had a strong presence in Egypt, and Ethiopia, which borders the Red Sea, had always been a loyal British ally. Eden stood up for Ethiopia against Italy because the contractual obligations with the League of Nations demanded it when Ethiopia was invaded by Italy. When Britain walked away from its obligation to Ethiopia, Eden resigned from the government.

Chamberlain and his like-minded Conservatives, who pointed to the autocratic emperorship of Ethiopia, rationalized their removal of sanctions against Italy. Eden recognized their reasoning for what it was—an excuse for expediency. Even if there were violations of human rights in Ethiopia, they paled when compared with those committed by the black-shirt Fascists, Mussolini's followers in Italy.

Those who, for short-run advantage, find it convenient to abandon a friend, an ally, a loyal customer, or a longtime client, may live to regret the decision in the long run. One should be careful of discarding a friend for whatever reason.

A consistent record of loyalty to friends and contractual fidelity—like name identification or reputation for service—are winning assets for major customers or clients. Churchill called such true blue types "foul weather friends."

A businessman in Philadelphia once told me that the reason he had welshed on a deal with a longtime business partner was the man's highly publicized, scandalous divorce. In diplomacy or business, one should not use human rights violations or a messy personal life as an excuse for not following through on a commitment.

In the 1940s, when Trujillo was the fascist military dictator of the Dominican Republic, President Franklin Roosevelt was urged to cut the trade and business ties with that country. Roosevelt answered, "I know he's a son-of-a-bitch, but he's our son-of-a-bitch."

IX

ALWAYS DO AT LEAST AS MUCH
FOR OUR FRIENDS
AS OUR ADVERSARIES DO FOR
OUR ENEMIES.

Nixon

The first American diplomat, Benjamin Franklin, said, "A friend in need is a friend in deed." Franklin supposedly recited that when imploring King Louis XVI to loan us French francs to pay for George Washington's Continental Army. Nixon, in this Ninth Commandment, applies a Realpolitik spin to the old truism about loyalty to friends. Between the lines he is advocating a foreign policy tenet that is a muted version of "My friend's enemies are my enemies!" Nixon was to have that principle tested in October 1973.

On the high Jewish holiday of Yom Kippur, Israeli prime minister Golda Meir was awakened in the middle of the night by a phone call from her top military aide. Syrian troops had invaded the Golan Heights, and Egyptian armies had crossed the Suez Canal.

Yom Kippur is the holiest day on the Jewish religious calendar. The country of Israel literally closes down. On this day, there are no newspapers, no television, no radio broadcasts, no public transportation, and all schools, shops, restaurants, cafés, and offices are closed for twenty-four hours. Even much of the army is given leave so that the soldiers can be with their families.

The Israeli prime minister addressed her nation on radio the next day, informing civilians of the invasion and the first casualties sustained. Then she added, "We are in no doubt that we shall prevail. We are convinced that this renewal of Egyptian and Syrian aggression is an act of madness." But after four days of heavy fighting, the unprepared Israelis had suffered heavy losses, including one fifth of their five-hundred-plane air force and one third of their 650 tanks.

Speaking to the Israeli Parliament on October 17, Golda Meir pointed her finger at the nation she believed had orchestrated this invasion:

> The hand of the Soviet Union is obvious in the equipment, the tactics, and the military doctrines that the Arab armies are trying to imitate and adopt. Above everything else, the Soviet Union's all-out support for Israel's enemies in the course of the war has been manifested in the airlift reaching our enemies' airfields and the ships calling at their ports.

Even though by the fifth day of the Yom Kippur War, Israelis had pushed the Syrians back across the 1967 cease-fire line and had checked Egyptian advance, the Israeli high command remained greatly alarmed.

As Golda Meir wrote in her memoirs, "I had to consider the possibility that the war would not be a short one and that we might find ourselves without planes, tanks, and ammunition we needed. We needed arms desperately."

Such help could come only from the United States. In Washington, President Nixon was beleaguered by his own crisis. The cover-up of campaign violations was beginning to unravel in what the press would popularize in the shorthand phrase "Watergate." In addition, Nixon's vice president, Spiro Agnew, had just resigned.

Despite his troubles, the President insisted on daily briefings by Kissinger, who only three weeks before had been appointed secretary of state. Cool to the idea of U.S. military assistance, Kissinger informed Nixon that the Israeli army needed little help in repelling the twin-pronged attacks of Syria and Egypt.

Kissinger believed that if heavy casualties were sustained by all the warring Mideast parties without U.S. involvement, the position of the United States in the Mideast would be strengthened. Unlike the USSR, who was aiding the Arab nations, the United States could emerge as the superpower whom both Arabs and Israelis could trust. In Kissinger's view, U.S. influence and leverage would thus be enhanced.

Nixon understood this rationale but weighed it against our diminished credibility as an ally if we did not stand by our friends. Israel had steadfastly supported the United States in its position on South Vietnam.

Nixon told Kissinger to "let the Israelis know we would replace their losses." Kissinger relented by allowing a trickle of aid.

Meanwhile, Prime Minister Meir was frantically calling her ambassador in Washington, Simcha Dinitz, on a daily basis to ask for immediate military shipments. "Simcha," she said to her former chief of staff, "tomorrow might be too late." As she wrote in her memoirs, "I knew Nixon was a friend of Israel and that I could rely on him."

Secretary of Defense James Schlesinger, who was also eager not to offend the Egyptians, would not allow El Al (Israeli) cargo aircraft to use U.S. military airports. He explained that "shipping any stuff into Israel blows any image we have as an honest broker." Kissinger reported to Nixon and his chief of staff Alexander Haig, who were vacationing in Key Biscayne, Florida, that "Defense wants [the Pentagon] to turn against Israel." Haig replied, "Sounds like Clements." William Clements, the deputy secretary of defense, was a Texas oilman who had many friends in the Arab world.

Kissinger, however, was playing a devious game. To Israelis, he was blaming the Defense Department for delay, but he implied to the Arabs and Soviets that the holdup was due to his own influence.

Kissinger assumed Israel would win quickly, and he opposed giving it major support that could make its victory too one-sided. "It would be best," Kissinger told Schlesinger, "if Israel came out a little ahead but got bloodied in the process, and if the U.S. stayed clean." Kissinger decided to withhold major deliveries to Israel as long as the Russians exercised restraint. The *Christian Science Monitor* echoed that belief, saying, "The arms shipment would wreck détente."

Yet shipment by the Soviets continued unabated. In one week, the Soviet airlift included 125 Antinov XII planes to Syria and 12 to Egypt.

In Washington, President Nixon began fuming at the slow-motion response of the Pentagon. The Chairman of the Joint Chiefs of Staff, Admiral Thomas Moorer, who was no friend to Israel, came up with a proposal to send only three of its C-5A transport aircraft on resupply missions. He explained this minimal response on the grounds that a larger number of American planes would offend the Arabs and Soviets.

Nixon was now rapidly losing his patience at the logistical obstacles thrown in the way of helping Israel. Although Israel needed every one of its pilots in the conflict, it was forced to send a few of them in transport planes to the United States. Furthermore, some of these planes had to fly all the way to Boeing in Seattle for some of their defense shopping lists. Finally, the Israeli planes were not permitted to land at the military air bases, including the closest one to Israel at Dover, Delaware. The Defense Department said it had no authority to ask U.S. civilian transport to help the Israelis. The Israelis could land only at civilian airports or the private airports of defense industries.

Nixon was especially angered when he learned that the five Phantom jets he had ordered sent to Israel three days earlier had not left America.

"Do it now!" Nixon snapped at Kissinger.

"I thought it was done," announced Kissinger. "But every day they [the Pentagon] find an excuse."

Nixon roared, "I'm pissed off about this business about not getting the planes through."

Overriding the advice of Secretary of State Kissinger and Defense Secretary Schlesinger, Nixon ordered an immediate airlift, the likes of which dwarfed the one to West Berlin in 1948. He told Schlesinger to stop worrying about the Soviets and Arabs. "We are going to get blamed just as much for three planes as three hundred." Nixon added that he would take full responsibility if the Arabs retaliated by cutting off oil supplies.

To Kissinger, Nixon said, "Use every one [plane] we have—everything that can fly."

In Israel, the effect of the airlift was electrifying. As the droning American transport planes filled the skies over Tel Aviv, cars stopped in the streets, apartment windows were opened, and people began to shout, "God bless America" and "Thank you, President Nixon." Flights landed every hour bringing an average of about five hundred tons of equipment and arms per day. In her memoirs, Golda Meir admits that she cried at a cabinet meeting the day the airlift started.

The mammoth airlift is an example of another Nixonian rule, which he did not include in his Ten Commandments. I once heard him refer to both Anthony Eden's failure in the

Suez and Kennedy's defeat at the Bay of Pigs: "Sometimes leaders are hesitant about executing strong and controversial measures in the belief that a less than full-hearted operation mutes criticism. When you once decide," said Nixon to a group of us, "go with all your might."

Nixon, against the recommendations of his cabinet, weighed in with all his might to aid Israel. Because of the airlift, Israel moved from the defensive to the offensive in its confrontation with the Syrians and Egyptians. Assured of continuing supplies, the Israeli armies unleashed twin-pronged attacks against its two foes. When the Soviets issued veiled military threats in response to Nixon's all-out involvement in Israel, Nixon put the United States on nuclear alert.

Golda Meir would later write, "Nixon ordered the U.S. alert on October 14, 1973, because détente or no, he was not about to give in to Soviet blackmail. It was, I think, a dangerous decision, a courageous decision, and a correct decision."

Nixon believed a country should stand up for its friends. The Soviets were steadily supplying their allies, thus Nixon's airlift to Israel equaled and exceeded what the USSR had given to Syria and Egypt. In an emotional meeting, Israeli ambassador Simcha Dinitz took Tricia and her husband, Ed Cox, aside and wept on Cox's shoulder. "President Nixon saved Israel." Nixon refused to allow our Cold War rival to do more for Israeli's foes than he would do for our friends.

Pericles

Hannah Milhous Nixon could read Greek as well as Latin. The former schoolteacher insisted that her son, Richard, take Latin in Whittier High School. Though Greek was not offered as an elective in either Whittier High School or Whittier College, ancient history was, and Richard, at the urging of his mother, studied the civilizations of Athens and Rome in both high school and college. Just as his mother checked on his Latin homework, so she quizzed him on his ancient history. Mrs. Nixon's favorite hero was Pericles, the elected Greek head of the first democracy. She transmitted that reverence to her son.

Pericles, who lived five centuries before Christ, may be said to have combined the assets of both George Washington and Abraham Lincoln. Like Washington, Pericles was an aristocratic general whose appearance radiated authority. His massive head atop a tall frame struck awe in listeners even before he opened his mouth. Yet like Lincoln, Pericles possessed the deal-making skills of a politician and the phrase-making art of a poet. His Funeral Address to the Athenians stands with the Gettysburg Address as the greatest of memorial addresses.

Yet the patrician Pericles affected to despise politics. When he resigned his military command to seek the leadership of his nation, he claimed to be reluctantly answering the call of duty. With some discreet manipulation of the "populist" party members in the Ecclesia—the legislative assembly of Athens— he was elected archon, or president.

For its art, drama, and verse, the society of Athens was the envy of the world, but its elected form of government invited suspicion and fear from neighboring countries. Today, democracies are considered more stable than dictatorships, but the reverse was true twenty-five centuries ago in the Greek islands.

Most of the other Hellenic states were oligarchies with leaders appointed by a cabal of the richest families. Sparta, the biggest of the Greek-speaking states, was more authoritarian than an oligarchy—it is considered by some the forerunner of fascism for its cult of the state and the military discipline it demanded of its citizenry. Each Spartan male was trained to be a soldier. In military might, Sparta was the colossus of the Peloponnesus. If Athens led in arts, Sparta dominated by arms.

The rivalry between Athens and Sparta was the Hellenic version of the twentieth-century "cold war." Pericles tried to position Athens against the military threat of Sparta by cultivating friendly relations with the other Greek states.

An uprising in the little island of Corcyra (now the island of Corfu), some 250 miles from Athens, presented a military opportunity for the state of Corinth, an ally of Sparta, to exploit. Of all the Greek states, Corinth was the closest to being a satellite of Sparta. Corcyra was the Grecian gateway to the West—to Sicily and Italy—and Corinth coveted that port. Sparta had virtually adopted Corinth because it needed the Corinth port that was the gateway through the Hellespont to the eastern Aegean Sea. If Corinth conquered and absorbed Corcyra, Sparta, through its closest ally, Corinth, would then have a gateway to both East and West.

The threatened Corcyra dispatched an ambassador to Athens to plea for military assistance. The envoy informed the members of the Athenian Ecclesia that Sparta was eager for war between Corinth and Corcyra. Sparta stood to gain if Corinth was victorious. The implication was that it was not to Athens's advantage to see a satellite of Sparta swallow up Corcyra.

The minister from Corcyra, however, recognized that Athens would be reluctant to commit an act that might invite military retaliation from Sparta. To that point, he argued, "Actually, you will not be breaking your truce [of nonaggression] with Sparta, for you will be only supporting us against Corinth." The Corcyrean delegate reminded the Athenian assembly of the long history of friendship between their city-state and Athens. The envoy argued that even though the nonaggression pact recently concluded with Sparta superseded former mutual defense arrangements with his country, the pact with Sparta did not preclude coming to the aid of Corcyra.

Then, in a direct plea to Archon Pericles, he said, "He [Pericles] should understand that this is in the self-interest not so much of Corcyra but Athens . . . for Corcyra is favorably advantaged as the gateway to Italy and Sicily to the West." In other words, if Athens helped Corcyra, it would have a friendly harbor, not only for trade but as a defense of its western flank.

When the news of the Corcyrean envoy to Athens was reported to Corinth, Corinth sent its ambassador to the Ecclesia to counter the Corcyrean arguments. "You of Athens have no military treaty with them," the ambassador announced, "and if they sought such an alliance, they should have come when they were in no danger and not after the fact."

The Corinthian envoy also warned them: "Don't be tempted by their offer of a naval alliance. You will be seen by other Greek states as a meddler into another state's politics."

Much of the Ecclesian assembly agreed with Corinth's argument that by aiding Corcyra, Athens would violate its own best interests. Pericles thought differently. "To allow the navy of Corcyra to be commandeered by Corinth would upset the delicate balance of power in the Aegean. Sparta could then take over the fleet of the defeated Corcyra to supplement its army." So Pericles ordered ships to be sent to Corcyra to help in its war against Corinth.

The first batch of ships was not enough to forestall a rout of the Corcyreans. Pericles then realized that Athens had to intervene directly to save the small island. Pericles himself led an armada of thirty Athenian ships to Corcyra to prevent a total seizure of the beleaguered state. When he arrived in the port of Corcyra, Pericles, from his ship, could overhear the Corinthian commander ordering his men, "Take all the Corcyreans and kill them."

Pericles answered with an ultimatum: "We are not beginning war, men of the Peloponnesus, nor are we breaking the treaty, but we have come to aid the Corcyreans here who are our allies. Sail on anywhere you wish, we will not stop you, but if you ever sail against Corcyra or by any place of theirs, we shall not allow it."

The Corinthian fleet had no desire to fight Athens, so it withdrew and sailed away. Pericles had rescued the Corcyreans from conquest. For years Sparta had been dispatching military aid to Corinth. Pericles, however, determined that Athens would not give less to its old ally when it was attacked by Sparta's junior partner, Corinth. In 450 B.C., Pericles may have been the first leader to prove a cardinal rule of statecraft: give aid to a friend when he is attacked by your adversary's ally.

Pericles understood the necessity of coming to the aid of a friend who is threatened by a satellite of its principal adversary. The reputation of loyalty, whether to a political ally, a friend, or business client, is credit in the bank. The failure to sustain that loyalty diminishes the credibility of a country or company.

X

NEVER LOSE FAITH. IN JUST CAUSE
FAITH CAN MOVE MOUNTAINS.
FAITH WITHOUT STRENGTH IS FUTILE,
BUT STRENGTH WITHOUT FAITH
IS STERILE.

Nixon

In his Tenth Commandment, Nixon follows a Biblical allusion with an aphorism that is both poetic and profound. He combines two of Churchill's observations, "It is bad for a nation to be without faith" and "A great principle only carries weight if it is associated with the movement of great forces." Although Nixon wrote this commandment at the end of his career, he revealed his grasp of this truth when he was just starting out as a politician.

In January 1946, the aspiring congressman addressed the Pomona Kiwanis Club on the topic of the Soviet Union. Nixon's critics would later spread the canard that he adopted his anti-Soviet position early in his career purely as a matter of political expediency. Actually, this was not a popular stance at the close of 1945. Russia was still considered our gallant ally, and its leader "Uncle Joe" Stalin. It would be three months before Winston Churchill would warn the world of an "iron curtain" descending upon Eastern Central Europe.

Nixon's harsh depiction of the regime of our recent

wartime partner was hardly in political fashion. Indeed, right after Churchill's Fulton address, President Truman offered to send the U.S. battleship *Missouri* to Russia to bring Stalin back and allow him to give his side of the Cold War story. Truman also ordered his secretary of state, Acheson, to snub Churchill by not attending a reception for him just after his Fulton speech. Indeed, Franklin Roosevelt's widow denounced Churchill as a "warmonger" for his blunt description of the Soviet Union and its expanding control of central and eastern Europe.

In early 1946, Alger Hiss was an esteemed, talented, and dedicated diplomat. In fact, the prestigious Carnegie Endowment for International Peace had just recruited Hiss as its head to bring some national clout to its foreign policy think tank in Washington. Also in the spring of 1946, a former tail-gunner sergeant named Joe McCarthy was testing the political waters in the Senate race in Wisconsin, where he sought and gained the state's Communist party endorsement in the Republican primary campaign.

This early postwar trust and affection for the Soviet Union belies the charge that Nixon's words against the Soviets were a ploy of political opportunism.

The same critics have also claimed that Nixon was a political adventurer without a party affiliation until he answered some newspaper advertisement seeking a Republican candidate for Congress. The truth is that Nixon, before the war, had been the president of the local Young Republicans. In the war, Nixon had sought out former Minnesota governor Harold Stassen for a Pacific Island meeting. Stassen, then a high officer in the navy who had been keynoter at the Republican Convention in 1940, was being mentioned as a possible candidate in 1948.

Nixon did not answer any ad. What he did was reply to a letter in which Herman Perry, a local civic leader and Republican activist in Orange County, who had long watched Nixon as a political comer, suggested he run for Congress.

Nixon appeared before a screening committee, clad in his lieutenant commander naval uniform. The thirty-three-year-old returning veteran radiated energy and commitment. He looked like the best choice to unseat the incumbent Congressman Jerry Voorhis and so was slated by the Republican Committee.

Nixon's first electioneering problem was recognition, for he was virtually unknown outside his hometown of Whittier. Perry immediately swung into action and called acquaintances, telling them that Dick Nixon, who was just getting out of the navy, was a good speaker and an ideal program choice for their group.

One of Nixon's first invitations to speak came from the Pomona Kiwanis, which met for a weekly Wednesday luncheon. Nixon was informed that the typical topics for this men's service club were local sports, community activities like the Boy Scouts, or possibly business topics such as citrus growing in the valley. The Kiwanis audience would be mostly local merchants, along with a few lawyers, doctors, dentists, and accountants. Since Nixon had been away in the war, they suggested that he might want to talk about his experiences in the South Pacific.

Nixon, however, selected a subject that would have been more suited for a banquet at a World Affairs Group of Los Angeles, or the Foreign Policy Association meeting in New York: the response of the Free World to the growing threat of the Soviet Union. He entitled it "The Challenge to Democracy," and it was a probing historical analysis of the Soviet threat to democratic values.

Nixon opened on a shocking note:

The history of Russia is a tragic story of war, starvation, torture, rape, murder, and slavery. They have never in all their history known as we Americans have the peaceful co-existence of neighboring states side by side with established boundaries. To them all foreigners are potential enemies. They have never known what it means to live in freedom. They have always been ruled by dictators.

Nixon then denounced Stalinism for the collectivization of farms that led to three million deaths in the Ukraine alone, and for its police state whose imprisonment and torture crushed all dissent and human rights.

When he addressed the imperialist ambitions of Soviet policy and the appropriate reply to it, Nixon's vision was prophetic:

Russia has now grabbed Estonia, Latvia, Lithuania, Eastern Poland, parts of Finland, Czechoslovakia and Romania. The Soviets do not need these parts of Europe. . . . Now the Soviet Government is strong and firmly entrenched, but it is weak in the light of history because it has set itself against the surge of mankind towards freedom and democracy.

So what have we to offer? We should not hesitate to help democratic elements in the states controlled by Soviet puppet governments. But we must not attack Russia on the grounds that it may attack us. This would reduce us to a moral level not far below theirs. Man cannot murder by becoming a murderer. We must use means that conform to the highest moral standards. The most legitimate use of force on earth is to gain time to permit the growth of moral ideas. But at some point we must stop Soviet imperialism. We must use our economic, political and military power. . . . We owe it to the world to hold the line for the growth of democratic ideals, to show how well our own democracy works here and to sell our ideas to the rest of the world and to the Russian people.

In other words, Nixon was arguing that it was not enough for America to be just anti-Communist. He believed that America had to prove the superiority of its democratic ideal or, as his Tenth Commandment would later express it, "Strength without faith is sterile." At the same time, in a line that foreshadowed "Faith without strength is futile," he argued for the buildup of economic and political power to hold the line until the Soviet system collapsed under the rottenness of its own system.

Only Nixon would have devoted so much reading of history and preparation to draft a major foreign policy address to such a minor audience. Only Nixon, among the congressional candidates a half century ago, had the wisdom to foresee that the Soviet Union would eventually crumble—provided America mobilized its deterrence of military might "to gain time to permit the growth of moral ideas."

The greatness of the Nixon foreign policy record owes much to his intellectual vision—together with imagination and discipline—to think and plan such a policy, and his political determination to implement it. In his fifty-year career as prophet, politician, president, and foreign policy elder statesman, Nixon was America's most consistent advocate for holding the line against Soviet expansionism.

Napoleon III

Ever since Edward Gibbon penned his epic *The Decline and Fall of the Roman Empire*, the collapse of great nations has been a favorite topic for historians. The fall of the Bourbon monarchy in the French Revolution of 1789; the collapse of the Manchu dynasty with the establishment of the Chinese Republic in 1912; and lately, of course, the toppling of the Iron Curtain and the Soviet Communist empire all bear testament to the truth that military might, in and of itself, cannot sustain a bad idea.

A few pages are not enough to depict the decades of slow rot in monarchies or totalitarian tyranny that made their subjects or citizens turn from disillusionment to despair and finally to the overturning of their hated regimes. What fits the purposes of this book is a historic case example that was so stupid in its conception that its regime died a quick death despite the might of its professional army. Such an absurd idea was Napoleon III's plan to plant a European monarchy in Mexico in 1864.

This Napoleon, unlike his uncle, was no genius. He may have had the Bonaparte charm, but he lacked judgment. Napoleon III was the son of Napoleon I's brother, whom the first Napoleon had installed on the throne of Holland.

At the age of twenty-eight, this new Napoleon made an abortive attempt against King Louis Philippe to return the Bonapartes to power in France. As a result, he was exiled. His first three months were spent in America—a short stay that may have fueled his New World fantasies. In addition, his grandmother, the Empress Josephine, was a native of the French island of Martinique. His mother, Queen Hortense, spent many years there as a young girl. Homesick for Europe and its culture, the young Napoleon finally managed to find a home in Switzerland. There he continued to feed his fascination for America by mapping plans for a canal in Nicaragua linking the two oceans. Yet his fantasies about America did not include a fondness for the Americans in the new North American republic. His distaste for the ruder elements of the American democracy was exceeded only by his disdain for the crudeness of their culture. He viewed the increasing dominance of the United States in Latin America as a rebuff to the civilized royal societies of Europe.

His attitude was ironic, since he owed his triumphant return to France to a democratic election. After the abdication of King Louis Philippe, he won the election of 1848 by more than five million votes and became president of France. Four years later, he overthrew the French Republic and proclaimed himself Napoleon III.

By the 1860s, he saw in Mexico an opportunity to realize his dream for the New World. He envisioned a monarchy that would act as a model for the other Latin American nations that had freed themselves from their Spanish rulers some decades before. An emperor with all the grace and culture of a royal court would make a striking contrast to the series of grubby politicians who became presidents of the United States.

In the forty years since Mexico had shaken off its Spanish yoke, the country had witnessed thirty-six different forms of government, including seventy-three presidents. In 1822, the Mexicans, under General Agustín de Iturbide, gained independence from Spain, and the soldier-liberator proclaimed himself emperor. Between Emperor Iturbide and President Benito Juárez, the recently ousted leader, Mexico was ruled by a series of corrupt caudillo regimes that masked themselves as republican governments.

In 1863, a coalition of grandee landowners and primates of
the Catholic Church had succeeded in overthrowing Juárez,
driving him to the northern mountains near Monterrey. The
result was a vacuum in Mexico City—the ideal circumstances
for Napoleon to carry out his vision. France, which he deemed
"the arm and soul of Latin civilization," could lift the New
World from the degradation of American democracy.

The pawn for his plan was Archduke Ferdinand Maximilian. This hapless Hapsburg was twenty-nine and out of work
when news reached him of the job opening for a monarch
in Mexico. In 1861, Maximilian wrote Napoleon III, offering
his appreciation of the honor Napoleon was arranging for
him. A cultured and humane romantic, Maximilian combined
the inconsistent creed of a political liberalism with a passion-
ate loyalty to his Austrian royal house. He had married the
seventeen-year-old Princess Charlotte, daughter of King
Leopold of Belgium, who was uncle of Queen Victoria. In
brains and ambition, she was her husband's superior. The
young couple lived near Trieste in Miramar in a palace that
overlooked the Adriatic Sea, where he served as governor-
general of Lombardy-Venetia, a royal sinecure that Emperor
Franz Joseph in Vienna had secured for his nephew, whom he
held in little esteem.

In Mexico, the time seemed ripe for the installing of a
Hapsburg heir. The Conservative party, with its allies in the
aristocracy, the army, and the church, was dominant. The
Liberal party, which had once given its full allegiance to
Juárez, was in disarray. Only Indian guerrillas in the northern
mountains supported the former president. With hardly any
resistance, General François Achille Bazaine led his French
troops into Mexico City. Perhaps if the United States had not
been embroiled in a civil war, the diplomatic protests of Lincoln's secretary of state might have taken the form of military

intervention in compliance with the Monroe Doctrine. The Confederacy, however, which was angling for recognition by Napoleon III, had given its implicit assent to a Maximilian monarchy.

In October 1863, a Mexican delegation led by Gutiérrez de Estrada arrived in Europe. Estrada had been a leader in the effort to oust Juárez. An aristocrat from an old Spanish family, Estrada was a royalist by conviction and had put himself in charge of recruiting a Hapsburg heir to rule Mexico. In Paris, the cabinet members of Napoleon III suggested that Estrada assume the title of president to make his tendering of the Mexican throne to Maximilian seem constitutional. The Mexican delegation traveled to Miramar in 1864 and issued a formal request to Maximilian to become emperor of Mexico. He accepted the offer as an expression of will from the Mexican people.

On the long crossing, Maximilian and Charlotte busied themselves with their first priority. They drafted a six-hundred-page book of court etiquette, outlining the canons and protocols that had been shaped during four centuries of the Hapsburg monarchs. The court code included such details as the difference in uniforms for upstairs and downstairs maids, the number of centimeters between the wine goblets and water glasses, and the hours and days for levees and receptions.

On May 28, 1864, Emperor Maximilian and Empress Charlotte landed at Veracruz. Charlotte cried as she noted the joyless faces of the crowds, while her husband tried to maintain his bravado. His Mexican hosts in the royal procession attempted to explain that the populace was only confused and had yet to appreciate the noble humanity of their new ruler. They promised the reception would be better when the imperial cortege reached Puebla.

The prediction proved true. Juan Nepomaceno, a Conservative, had laid careful plans for a cordial reception in this stronghold of aristocratic grandees.

In Mexico City, the Emperor moved into the former presidential palace. In the very first days, he printed and promulgated the rules of court etiquette. He also published a court newspaper in French—*L'ère nouvelle*—that reported, among other things, the receptions, levees, and cultural events he attended.

Maximilian may have been familiar with the arts of poetry but not of politics. In the court he often supervised theatrical productions. Yet it was statecraft, not stagecraft, he required to build support in ruling a suspicious populace.

Maximilian was infirm in purpose and irresolute in policy. He was a contradiction in terms—a royalist by breeding and a liberal by beliefs. He might have succeeded, at least in the short term, if he had danced with the people who had brought him to the ball—the Conservatives. Yet he distrusted the Church and alienated the grandees by refusing to undo the land reform of the previous Liberal president Juárez.

His moderation did not win over the republican Liberals but only antagonized the Conservatives, his original base of support. With the upper classes disillusioned and the lower classes distrustful, Maximilian proceeded to alienate the middle classes—the merchants and shopkeepers in the cities and towns—by running up a huge deficit. His building projects, together with the high costs of maintaining court life, had caused expenses to rocket to forty million pesos by September 1865, with revenues of only seventeen million.

Despite the presence of French troops to bolster him, Maximilian's regime was cracking. If the fissure widened, soon he would become Humpty Dumpty, with "all the king's horses and all the king's men" unable to repair him.

Back in Paris, Napoleon III was losing patience with Maximilian and interest in his grand design for the New World. The defeat of the Confederacy in April 1865 now made available mobilized Union troops to put teeth in Secretary of State Seward's diplomatic protests.

Napoleon III was in no position to resume his grand design. General Bazaine pleaded for reinforcements for his forty thousand troops in Mexico, when in fact, Napoleon III needed those forty thousand in Europe. The French emperor already had deployed eighty thousand soldiers to Algeria and twenty thousand to Rome.

Since an aggressive and acquisitive Prussia under Bismarck was an increasing threat on France's northern border, Napoleon hoped to cut the strings of his puppet pawn, Maximilian, and bring back the much-needed troops. The French sent word to Washington that if the United States would give their recognition to Maximilian's government, they would withdraw their troops from Mexico.

The imminence of the French withdrawal threw Maximilian into a panic. He acceded to the advice of the Conservatives and in 1865 issued a death edict for any opponents of his emperorship. The death penalty for gun-toting Juárez Republicans pleased the French generals but not its diplomats, who anxiously watched relations with the United States deteriorate.

On the advice of the diplomats, Napoleon III announced on January 22, 1866 that France was preparing to bring her troops back from the New World. While Paris clung to the illusion that the Mexican empire would somehow survive evacuation, the Conservatives in Mexico knew better. They advised Maximilian to abdicate. He might have done so if it had not been for his wife, Charlotte. She persuaded him to continue, on the promise that she would cross the ocean to win back support from Napoleon III.

In Paris, Napoleon III told her that the French army would

stay on until February 1867, provided Maximilian would abdicate then and come back with the returning French troops. Overcome with despair and disillusionment, Charlotte went to see the Pope in September 1866 at the Vatican, where her troubled mind gave way. She struggled with mental illness until her death in Belgium sixty-one years later in 1927.

In Mexico City, Maximilian postponed his abdication after learning of his wife's failure and subsequent collapse. He now faced military attack. Juárez's guerrilla forces were assembling for the march to the capital as the French army moved to Veracruz for its departure.

Maximilian repaired to the stronghold at Querétaro, some 160 miles north of Mexico City. There his desperate overtures were rebuffed.

The Republicans, increasing their forces daily, began the siege of Querétaro in March 1867. It ended sixty-seven days later when the Emperor was captured. He was court-martialed for treason and sentenced to death. He never proved himself more royal than in the way he faced execution on June 19, 1867. He shook hands with his firing squad and said in Spanish, "You are soldiers and are rightly following your orders. I only ask you to do your job well—shoot cleanly—so that my widow does not receive a disfigured corpse."

Maximilian was a most improbable monarch—an Austrian prince, propped up by a French army, attempting to rule a Latin American republic. Napoleon III had tried to plant the potted flower of monarchy in the hostile clime of a republic. Even with French troops and some conservative support, the idea withered rapidly as guerrilla incursions mounted.

In Brussels, Charlotte lived on with her impaired mind unaware that Maximilian had been executed. Every spring for six decades as the crocuses signaled the arrival of the new season, Empress Charlotte would announce, "It is time to pack up. We are sailing for Mexico City." The staff would then load up the suitcases in front of her, only to dismantle the packing privately. Charlotte was crazy, but the grand design of Napoleon III to export a monarchy to Mexico that would spread to other Latin American republics was just as insane.

It is a lesson in politics as well as business: a bad idea, despite the assets of capital and a management team, cannot be forced on an unwilling buyer. Power, without faith and trust, is sterile. Mexico was an unwilling buyer for the Maximilian monarchy. Napoleon III, however, never possessed real faith in his royal plan for the New World because he never followed through. It was more whim than vision, more a scheme than a dream of the true believer.

The communism that Nixon saw being brutally enforced in Russia and eastern Europe had no lack of true believers. Right after the war, there were many intellectuals, both abroad and here, who admired the Marxist ideals of communism and closed their eyes to the brutality of Stalin. Nixon foresaw that truth about the evils of communism would eventually emerge and support for the regime would in time erode. In other words, communism, despite the iron might of its army and secret police, would collapse in large part for lack of faith.

ADDENDUM

Having laid down these rules, I would also suggest that the President keep in his desk drawer, in mind but not out of sight, an Eleventh Commandment: When saying "always" and "never," always keep a mental reservation; never foreclose the unique exception; always leave room for maneuver. A President always has yet to be prepared for what he thought he would never do.

This "Eleventh Commandment" is more of an addendum than an axiom. Nixon wrote it not so much as a rule but as an exception to the ten rules.

The first Ten Commandments are like the bold block-lettered statements of hornbook law in legal textbooks. These are rules that condense in short sentences the case decisions of common law jurisprudence (i.e., "Ignorance of the law is no defense"; "Insanity is the inability to know right from wrong"; "Possession is nine points of the law"; "Caveat emptor" [buyer beware]). Yet lawyers who study for the bar realize mere knowledge of the thousands of precepts in torts, contracts, and criminal law is not enough to pass examinations. The would-be lawyer has to know the case material that would both explain the situational context and that might except its application.

Nixon's postscript is a plea to future leaders not to let themselves be straitjacketed into dogmatics. Nixon believed that too often the doctrinaire diminishes his field of performance and constrains his capacity for action.

In referring to President Eisenhower's hobby as a "Sunday artist," Nixon once said, "General Eisenhower never painted by numbers, and there's no simple formula for foreign policy either."

Nixon had a disdain for the ideological right as well as the left—although he concealed it more for the former. As he said once to me, "Jamie, I've never believed one 'ism' could solve all problems." The true believer, he thought, deceives himself when he thinks of everything in terms of black and white. He agreed with Churchill, who said of such ideologues: "Perfection is the enemy of progress," and "the fanatic is one who can't change his mind and can't change the subject."

"Zealotry," said Nixon, "makes for better speeches than solutions." Wearing blinders limits the flexibility of choice and the possibility of finding answers to problems. Ideological crusaders produce more rhetoric than results.

The "liberal" thinking Nixon disdained was the "cookie cutter" version with its stereotyped answers. Actually, there were many who would be described as left-of-center "liberals" on Nixon's White House staff. Pat Moynihan, Len Garment, and Jean Moyer, former president of Tufts, are a few that come to mind.

It has been argued by many, including Tom Wicker of *The New York Times,* that Nixon was the most progressive president in either party since Lyndon Johnson. Nixon's massive funding for cancer research, his commitment to the arts, his establishment of the Environmental Protection Agency, his beginning of "affirmative action" in the Philadelphia Plan, his end to the draft, his successful drive to extend the vote to eighteen-year-olds, and his desegregation in the Deep South are testament to that opinion.

Unlike some Republicans today, Nixon was not hostile to government itself—only to the bureaucracy, its needless waste, and the higher taxes that an unbridled government can generate. Neither was he hostile to liberal objectives, only to the liberal ideology that was rigid and biased.

Nixon himself was a conservative, but his conservatism was instinctive, not ideological, and in his study of history, he saw that great leaders did not let themselves be trapped by their ideology. To Nixon, neither the budget balancers nor "supply siders" had all the answers to our problems at home. Similarly, neither the economic isolationism of a Perot nor the international moralism of a Carter would make the world abroad safe and stable.

Great leaders understand when situations invite decisions that might run against the very grain of their background and values. In the sixteenth century, Henry of Navarre was a Calvinist Protestant. He raised and led armies to topple the French king who persecuted Navarre's fellow Huguenots. When Henry seized Paris, he found himself at the head of a nation divided by the deep-seated enmities of Catholic and Protestant sections of the population. He soon realized that the only way he could bring stability to his country was by converting to Catholicism. He would satisfy the Catholics, but he would ensure that there would be no persecution of Protestants. "Paris," said he, "was worth a Mass."

Benjamin Franklin considered himself an Englishman. He had rejoiced at the coronation of King George III—the first English king in half a century who could actually speak English. Franklin spent his formative years learning and mastering the craft of printing in London and he came to love the infinite variety and challenges of the English capital city. He cherished his English heritage, which granted him rights as a free man through such titled deeds of liberty as the Magna Carta, the petition of right, and the writ of habeas corpus.

In Philadelphia, Franklin became a general in the Pennsylvania militia during the English war against the French. When Franklin traveled to London in 1774 to lobby against Parliament's new tax laws, he was confident he could persuade his fellow Englishmen to amend the laws because of their common language and heritage. He said upon arriving that "rebellion against the Crown was unthinkable."

After two years in London, during which the breach between the motherland and her Atlantic colonies had widened beyond repair, Franklin wrote to Charles Thompson, the Secretary of the Continental Congress, proclaiming that, "The sun of liberty is setting; it is time to light the candle of enterprise." He left Britain to play a major role in drafting a document for independence.

Thomas Jefferson founded his party on states' rights and fervent opposition to an expanding federal government. "That government which governs best governs least" was his legendary maxim. He had opposed President Washington when he established a national bank. The bigger the government became, he believed, the more likely it would become a tool for repression and tyranny.

Yet Jefferson's deeply held opinions were jolted by a rare opportunity in 1803, when Napoleon wanted to sell the lands west of the Mississippi. The Emperor needed money to finance his war against Britain, and the faraway Louisiana territory was expendable.

The massive outlay of over $25 million for the Louisiana Purchase in 1803 went against the very fiber of Jefferson's limited government philosophy, but he could not foreclose that unique exception. He was a plantation farmer who distrusted the merchant and banking classes of the city, and the Louisiana Purchase offered the chance to open up farms of the future and to extend the then seaboard United States westward.

In 1855, Abraham Lincoln was one of the first political leaders in Illinois to join the just-emerging Republican Party. A Whig who had served one term in Congress ten years before, Lincoln had been recruited by "anti-Nebraskans" to debate Stephen Douglas at a state fair. Senator Douglas, a renowned orator, was the advocate and chief sponsor of popular sovereignty—a law allowing states to choose by referendum to be either "free" or "slave." The new Republican Party, formed by these "anti-Nebraskans," opposed the extension of slavery in the territories.

In 1860, Lincoln was elected as the nation's first Republican president. Yet in 1864, he faced a difficult reelection campaign as the Union Army advance stalled. General Robert E. Lee had survived the defeat in Gettysburg, and a series of Confederate victories increased the likelihood that Britain and France—who had economic reasons for wanting the Union to lose—might recognize the Confederacy.

Whereas the South depended on international trade for their exports of cotton, the North had always been protectionist. British and French diplomats argued that the conflict was not so much a civil war as a sectional war and that recognition of the Confederacy was a realistic option because the North and South could never live together under one government.

The Republican Lincoln dared to do the unthinkable. He chose a Democrat to be his running mate. He summoned to the executive mansion a confidential and loyal political friend, A. H. McClure, a Philadelphia lawyer, and told him he was going to dump Hannibal Hamlin, his current vice president, for Governor Andrew Johnson of Tennessee.

When McClure questioned the decision, Lincoln replied, "We are trying to stave off recognition of the Confederacy by Britain as well as France. Over there, they don't understand what the number two man in our government really does. If we have Johnson, a Democrat who's from a southern state, we are proving that the South is coming back to the Union, and a southerner as Vice President shows our country is not just a northern government, but a national administration."

For the purposes of the 1864 presidential election, Lincoln changed the name of the Republican Party to the Union

Party. Lincoln and Johnson were victorious, and the European nations did not recognize the Confederacy. Lincoln, one of our greatest politicians as well as presidents, showed that sometimes the restraints of party and ideology have to be broken to achieve success.

One of Nixon's favorite historical figures was Benjamin Disraeli. Disraeli, who was Jewish in ancestry, had risen to the head of the Conservative Party, nicknamed the Tories. In the early seventeenth century, the typical Tory was an aristocratic landowner who believed in high church and espoused high tariffs against European wheat. He was a country squire who saw himself as a spokesman for the rural community that distrusted the Liberals as merchants of materialism. A Tory viewed the brokers and financiers from London, the shippers and traders from Liverpool, or the factory owners from Manchester and Leeds, as threats to traditional English values.

As the population in the mill city towns swelled with the influx of migrants from the country, Disraeli predicted that the Tories would have problems maintaining a majority in the House of Commons. While the Liberal Party typically championed parliamentary reform, the Tories had always relished their role as custodians of the status quo. But Disraeli—in a heretical move—proposed outflanking the Liberals by enacting legislation that would widen the voting franchise to those who were not strictly property owners. With this action, Disraeli and the Tories, for the first time, reached out to city dwellers. Disraeli correctly assumed that the newly enfranchised voters would turn to the Tories. Disraeli, as prime minister, was willing to do "what he thought he would never do."

Imaginative in concept and breathtaking in its sweep, Disraeli with this reform said, "we dished the Whigs." Nixon and his domestic affairs adviser, Pat Moynihan, had both read Blake's biography of Disraeli. When Nixon sent up to Congress Moynihan's "negative income" tax proposal in 1971 for ending welfare, he proclaimed, "This will dish the Democrats." The Democratic leaders of Congress, perhaps fearing the appeal of such a reform to their black constituency, buried the proposal. The bill would have freed ghettos from the shackles of bureaucracy while still providing a means of subsistence. At the same time, it would have dismantled the network of welfare workers, which wielded strong influence in big-city Democratic strongholds.

The greatest British prime minister in history, Winston Churchill, was also a Conservative. He had etched his name in the annals of history, not just for his performance in leading Britain in the war against Germany, but for his lonely prophecies about the threat of Germany before the war. Churchill was the only statesman who had served in the cabinet in two wars against Germany. Yet only months after Germany surrendered, Churchill would rock the world with his addresses at The Hague, in the Netherlands and in Zurich, Switzerland. He asserted that Germany should have a major role in the rebuilding of Europe and that the cooperation and unity of Europe's two largest nations, Germany and France, was essential. In these two speeches, Churchill knew that only he had the world stature to offer a vision of a united Europe that transcended ancient enmities and historic prejudices.

When the French people returned General Charles de Gaulle to the presidency in 1958, he faced a looming conflict in Algeria. As a professional soldier, he was backed strongly in the election by the army and its veterans. De Gaulle was no stranger to North Africa—he had served there both before and during World War II. To those who had lived in Algeria for three or four generations, the insurrection by the Arab and Muslim Algerians was a threat to the French society and civilization they cherished, and they had enlisted de Gaulle in their political cause.

Charles de Gaulle embodied for many the glory of France, its history and civilization. Although he was a sphinx on the subject of Algeria during the campaign, it was widely believed that he would not turn his back on the French population there.

Upon election de Gaulle decided that radical measures were required to ensure a future for France. Despite warnings from his own Gaullists and right-wing supporters, he believed that the amputation of the limb of French North Africa was the only way to save the body of France, which had been sapped and debilitated by the ongoing Algerian conflict. His aides warned him he would be branded as a traitor by some of his most loyal followers and surely risk assassination. But de Gaulle knew that as the French hero of World War II who headed the liberation parade into Paris, only he could per-suade the nation that withdrawal from Algeria was an honor-able course. Despite the unpopularity of the action with the military and the right, de Gaulle's prestige made the indepen-dence of Algeria possible in 1962.

De Gaulle served as both a model and a mentor for Nixon. Like Alexander, another great general, de Gaulle didn't try to untie the Gordian knot that was Algeria. Instead, he cut it cleanly with his sword. He possessed the daring and fearless-ness to do the unthinkable—the severing of Algeria from France—even when it meant the alienation and enmity of some of his strongest supporters.

Nixon would likewise endanger his own conservative base and risk the charge of betrayal from his faithful friend and ally Generalissimo Chiang Kai-shek in Taiwan when he approached the Communist revolutionary Mao. The example of de Gaulle in Algeria stiffened Nixon's resolve to reach out to the Communist People's Republic of China. De Gaulle had suggested that Nixon consider such a policy reversal, and when Nixon was preparing for his trip to China, de Gaulle sent his most loyal aide, André Malraux, to see him.

Malraux told Nixon, "You will be like the sixteenth-century explorers venturing into the unknown with faith in the rightness of the voyage but without sure knowledge of its outcome." Nixon, whose diligence in uncovering Hiss, whose courage in facing down Communist mobs in Caracas, and whose confrontation in the kitchen with Khrushchev had brought him the adulation of the anti-Communist right, now girded himself to do what his political friends and foes in America never expected. He did not "foreclose the unique exception."

In my book *The Wit and Wisdom of Winston Churchill*, one story particularly caught Nixon's fancy. When Hitler invaded Russia in June 1941, Churchill recommended aid to the Soviets. He was asked how he could justify that approach in the light of his anti-Bolshevik record going back to 1917, when he proposed sending British forces to the White Russians to help in their fight with the Communist revolutionaries. Churchill replied, "If Hitler invaded the realms of Hell, I might make some favorable reference to the Devil in the House of Commons."

Like Churchill and de Gaulle, Nixon was prepared to do the unthinkable to achieve the ultimate objective of making a safer world. It is not only in government that the real leader may find he has to take a course that "he thought he would never [have to] do." Over the last few decades, CEOs of corporations in steel or tobacco found they had to diversify to survive. Similarly, heads of long-standing family businesses have recently chosen, for economic reasons, to go public. Companies that have been based in one city throughout their history sometimes pull up stakes and move on. In all these cases, the course that the leader thought he would never consider when he assumed the helm became the only option.

EPILOGUE

Richard Nixon drew on his career as a corporate lawyer, world statesman, and student of history to craft the ten principles elucidated in this book.

His Ten Commandments of Statecraft apply not only to negotiations at the summit level but also to our everyday dealings in business and trade.

The forging of a framework for peace and stability between nations may be the stuff of history books, but the nuts and bolts of the statesman's tools are no different from those of the lawyer or business executive. A treaty, after all, is only a contract between nations.

The successful bargainer—whether a diplomat, merchant, or lawyer—cannot be vague in his objective, impatient with details, or infirm in resolve. Readers with many years in the business arena may find nothing unusual or startling in the Nixon rules. Perhaps they will only confirm the lessons of their own successes and failures. Nonetheless, what is extraordinary is Nixon's distillation of his vast experience as a leader and negotiator into ten simple but profound precepts.

INDEX

185

Nicolson, Harold, 85
Nixon (Aitken), 35, 110
Nixon, Edward (brother), 22
Nixon, Frank (father), 21–22
Nixon, Hannah (mother), 21–22, 46,
    154–55
Nixon, Julie (daughter), 113
Nixon, Mudge, Rose, Guthrie and
    Alexander, 91
Nixon, Richard M.:
    ancient history studied by, 154–55
    baseball enjoyed by, 19
    childhood, 21–22
    first election of, 159–63
    funeral of, 15, 121
    on hesitant leadership, 154
    on ideologues, 174
    intellectual challenge relished by,
        16–17
    magnanimity of, 121
    naval duty of, 22, 126
    New York Bar exam of, 26
    place in history as concern of,
        19–20
    as "policy wonk," 22–23, 30
    as progressive, 174–75
    reading of, 19–20, 113, 163
    in retirement, 15–18, 19
    "secret" slush fund of, 30–31
    speechwriting by, 18
    tour d'horizon talks of, 25
Nixon Doctrine, 137

Oakes, John B., 95
"October surprise," 106
Oswald, Henry, 101
Ottoman Empire, 114–19, 140
Oxford, Margaret, 87

Pakistan, 61, 63
Palestine, 140
Palmer, Alan, 66
Paris, Treaty of (1783), 97–104
Pericles, 154–58

Perot, H. Ross, 175
Perry, Herman, 160–61
Podgorny, Nikolay Viktorovich, 48
Poland, 69, 72, 94
Polk, James K., 55
Pomona Kiwanis Club, 159–63
Portsmouth Conference, 21
preparation, 29–44
    for Churchill's meeting with Roo-
        sevelt, 40–43
    fact-finding and, 44, 101
    Franklin and, 101–3
    national dimensions of, 35–39
    as Nixon's equalizer, 30
    for Nixon's 1946 Soviet Union
        address, 163
    for Nixon's 1959 Soviet Union
        visit, 31–35
    as strategic planning, 43–44
Price, Ray, 17
Prince, The (Machiavelli), 18
Prussia, 68–73, 169

Reagan, Ronald, 18, 97, 133
Real War, The (Nixon), 17
Reminiscences (MacArthur), 128–29,
    131
Reston, James, 79, 111
Rhyne, Charles, 23
Ribbentrop, Joachim von, 81
Richard Nixon Museum and
    Library, 18
Robb, Linda Johnson, 121
Rockingham, Charles Watson-
    Wentworth, marquis of, 101
Rogers, William, 63n, 107
Roosevelt, Eleanor, 15, 160
Roosevelt, Franklin, 57
    Churchill's meeting with, 40–43
    on distinguishing between friends
        and enemies, 147
    Munich Conference and, 83–84,
        85
    Nixon on, 14

Roosevelt, Theodore, 41, 45
Nixon's admiration for, 21
Rusk, Dean, 37
Russia, Imperial, 68–73, 114–19
Russo-Japanese War, 21
Russo-Turkish War, 87, 114–19

Sadat, Anwar, 122–26, 136
Safire, William, 34
Salisbury, Harrison, 34
Salisbury, Robert Cecil, Lord, 115
SALT (Strategic Arms Limitation
Talks), 37–39, 58
SALT (Strategic Arms Limitation
Talks) II, 96
Sandburg, Carl, 19
San Jacinto, battle of, 54
San Stefano, Treaty of, 114–19
Santa Anna, Antonio López de,
50–56
Saudi Arabia, 136, 137
Saxony, 69, 71, 72
Schlesinger, James, 151, 153
"scorched earth" policy, 125–26
Seven Years' War, 102
Seward, William, 166, 169
Shah of Iran, 135–39
Sharon, Ariel, 123–24
Sheehan, Edward, 125
Shelburne, Sir William Petty, earl of,
101–2
Sherman, William, 125
Singapore, 134
Six Crises (Nixon), 78
Six-Day War, 124
Smathers, George, 30
Snow, Edgar, 61–62
Solomon, king of Israel, 75, 144
Somaliland, 140
Sorenson, Ted, 29
Soviet Union:
Carter and, 94–97, 138
Churchill on, 24, 35–36, 105,
159–60, 181

collapse of, 163, 164
Far Eastern Commission and, 131
Nixon's 1946 address on, 159–63,
171
1972 summit meeting with, 35–39,
45–49, 55, 58, 65
Nixon's 1959 visit to, 31–35
and opening of China, 37–38, 46,
57–64, 92–97
Yom Kippur War and, 122–16,
150–54
Spain, 70, 72, 98, 165
Sparta, 155–58
Sputnik, 33
Stalin, Joseph, 57, 159, 171
Stassen, Harold, 160
State Department, U.S., 37, 58–61,
77, 92, 128
Stevenson, Adlai, 31
Sullivan, John, 125
Syria, 137, 140, 149–54

Taft, Robert, 126
Taiwan, 59, 60, 76, 92–93, 96–97,
134
Talleyrand, Charles Maurice de,
69–73
Texas, 50–56
Theodore Roosevelt Centennial
Commission, 21
Thieu, Nguyen van, 110–13, 134
Thompson, Charles, 176
Time, 62
totalitarians vs. authoritarians,
133–34
Travis, William, 53
triangularization, 60, 92–93, 108
Trujillo Molina, Rafael Leónidas, 147
Truman, Harry S., 15, 19, 32, 113,
127, 160
Turkey, 114–19

United Nations, 141
Unruh, Jesse, 44

DATE DUE